PLAINS NATIVE AMERICAN LITERATURE

Globe
Fearon

Upper Saddle River,
New Jersey

Executive Editor: Virginia Seeley

Project Editor: Kathleen Findorak

Contributing Editor: Ingrid Washinawatok

Art Director: Nancy Sharkey

Cover Design: Richard Puder Design

Interior Design: Joan Jacobus

Production Manager: Winston Sukhnanand

Desktop Specialist: José López

Marketing Manager: Elmer Ildefonso

Photo Research: Omni Photo Communications, Inc.
Cover: Prairie Fire, by Blackbear Bosin, *Philbrook Museum of Art,* Tulsa
Oklahoma

Literature and art acknowledgments can be found on pages 150–151.

Printed in the United States of America.
 4 5 6 7 8 9 10   04 03 02 01 00

ISBN: 0-835-90535-7

CONTENTS

UNIT 1: ORAL TRADITION   2

The First Cure   4
    as told through John G. Neihardt
       An excerpt from the autobiography
       Black Elk Speaks

Madonna Swan: A Lakota Woman's Story   12
    as told through Mark St. Pierre
       An excerpt from the autobiography
       Madonna Swan: A Lakota Woman's Story

Remaking the World   30
    as told by Leonard Crow Dog
       A folk tale from the anthology
       American Indian Myths and Legends

Focus on Writing   36

UNIT 2: NONFICTION   38

The School Days of an Indian Girl   40
    by Zitkala-Ša
       An excerpt from the biography
       American Indian Stories

**We've Got to Have Commitment
So Strong. . . . .**   48
    by John Trudell
       A speech

Focus on Writing   54

UNIT 3: FICTION   56

House Made of Dawn   58
    by N. Scott Momaday
       An excerpt from the novel
       House Made of Dawn

The Warriors   70
    by Anna Lee Walters
       A short story

Focus on Writing   88

UNIT 4: POETRY   90

Section 1: Reflections   92

The Man from Washington   93
   by James Welch

Indian Boarding School: The Runaways   94
   by Louise Erdrich

Extinction   95
   by Lance Henson

Morning Once More   96
   by Joy Harjo

Section 2: Living in Two Worlds   98

Remember   99
   by Joy Harjo

Calumet Early Evening   100
   by Annette Arkeketa West

Grandmother   101
   by Paula Gunn Allen

Driving in Oklahoma   102
   by Carter Revard

Focus on Writing   104

UNIT 5: DRAMA   106

49   108
   by Hanay Geiogamah
      A play

Focus on Writing   148

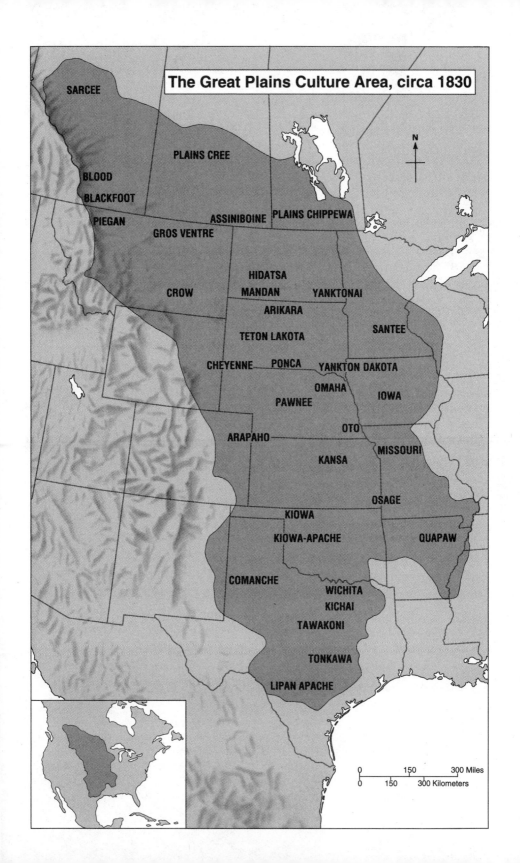

The Great Plains Culture Area, circa 1830

N

SARCEE

PLAINS CREE

BLOOD

BLACKFOOT

PIEGAN

ASSINIBOINE   PLAINS CHIPPEWA

GROS VENTRE

CROW

HIDATSA

MANDAN   YANKTONAI

ARIKARA

TETON LAKOTA   SANTEE

CHEYENNE   PONCA   YANKTON DAKOTA

OMAHA   IOWA

PAWNEE

OTO

ARAPAHO

MISSOURI

KANSA

OSAGE

KIOWA

KIOWA-APACHE   QUAPAW

COMANCHE

WICHITA

KICHAI

TAWAKONI

TONKAWA

LIPAN APACHE

0   150   300 Miles

0   150   300 Kilometers

Titles of literature are placed in the time box to reflect, when possible, the historical time or event about which the selections are written.

1830 Indian Removal Act

Black Elk Speaks ▼
1863 Black Elk is born.

1869 The first transcontinental railroad crosses the Plains. The Union Pacific and Central Pacific join up in Utah.

1876 Black Elk witnesses the Battle of Little Bighorn.

The School Days of an Indian Girl ▼
Indian Boarding School: The Runaways ▼
1879–1918 Carlisle Indian School: Native American children are sent to government boarding schools to be Americanized.

1881 The last of the Plains nations are exiled to reservations.

Extinction ▼
1885 The last of the great buffalo herds is killed.

Remember ▼
1887 Kiowa perform Oak Creek Sun Dance. The Sun Dance was later banned by government agent E.E. White in an effort to suppress Native American religious traditions.

1890 Federal troops massacre 350 Lakota men, women, and children at Wounded Knee thus putting an end to the Ghost Dance ceremony.

1924 Native Americans are given U.S. citizenship.

Madonna Swan: A Lakota Woman's Story ▼
The Warriors ▼
1930s Drought on the Great Plains causes devastation.

1941–1945 World War II: More than 25,000 Native Americans serve in the U.S. armed forces.

1968 The American Indian Movement (AIM) is founded.

House Made of Dawn ▼
1969 N. Scott Momaday is awarded the Pulitzer Prize for literature.

Remaking the World ▼
1973 Leonard Crow Dog and other AIM members along with 200 Oglala occupy Wounded Knee for 71 days.

We've Got to Have Commitment So Strong ▼
1973–1979 John Trudell serves as National Chairman of AIM.

1978 Indian Child Welfare Act passed to help preserve Native American heritage. Law restricts adoptions of Native American children by non Native American families.

Morning Once More ▼
1978 American Indian Religious Freedom Act upholds Native American rights to practice their religions and protect ceremonial grounds.

The Man from Washington ▼
Extinction ▼
1980 U.S. Supreme Court awards Lakota nation $105 million as compensation for Black Hills land. Lakota reject award.

49 ▼
1987 American Indian Dance Theater formed. Hanay Geiogamah becomes its Artistic Director.

Driving in Oklahoma ▼
1990 U.S. Census Bureau reports that Oklahoma has highest population of Native Americans in the country.

1990 One hundred year anniversary of Wounded Knee is commemorated. Chief Big Foot's ride and Ghost Dance reenacted.

1993 The United Nations celebrates the Year of the Rites of the Indigenous People.

DEAR STUDENT,

All of the cultures that make up the United States have played an important role in shaping the history of this country. In the following pages you will read literature by the Plains Native Americans. As you read their stories, speeches, plays, poems, and folk tales, reflect on the similarities and differences that make up these varied peoples.

The literature is organized into five units. Each unit is a special form of literature. The first unit is rooted in oral tradition. In oral tradition, people of a culture pass on through the spoken word their beliefs, values, and experiences through stories, songs, and personal accounts. Many of these stories, songs, and personal accounts are eventually written down by translators. The second unit presents nonfiction that emphasizes the personal experiences of the writers. The third unit consists of fictional stories, the basis of which can be found in the cultural roots of the writers. The fourth unit presents poetry that reflects the cultural issues that the writers encounter in their personal experiences. The literature in the fifth unit presents a drama that brings a modern Plains culture to life through words and songs.

The book also features a map that highlights the homelands of the Plains Native Americans. A time box provides information about historical events that occurred during the time period in which each selection is set.

As you read, think about the words. The messages come from many cultures that have endured great tragedies. Their people, though, write about their sufferings with dignity and in an expressive style. The experiences of the Plains Native Americans not only show us what makes their cultures special but also help to highlight the commonality of all cultures.

UNIT I

ORAL TRADITION OF THE PLAINS NATIVE AMERICANS

Oral tradition refers to the process of passing down sayings, songs, tales, and religious and spiritual beliefs from one generation to the next by word of mouth. Because early Native Americans did not have a written language, they relied on the oral communication of stories as a way of passing on the traditions of their culture. In some nations, the person with the best memory and the most imaginative skill became the "keeper" of that nation's history, songs, and myths.

Folk tales were an important part of the social and cultural life of Native Americans, regardless of their nation. Through the talent of a good storyteller, Native Americans could be carried away to an imaginary world. The dramatic effect was not only derived from the tale itself, but also from the various methods the storyteller used, such as the repetition of incidents and images.

The literature you are about to read is rooted in Native American oral tradition. Each selection reveals the values and beliefs of the speaker's culture and uses the methods of oral communication. The first selection, from *Black Elk Speaks,* tells the story of an Oglala medicine man who discovered his healing powers through nature. Next, the author Mark St. Pierre introduces you to Madonna Swan and retells how she learned the values of the Lakota from her extended family. The last selection, "Remaking the World," a folk tale told by Leonard Crow Dog, explains the creation of the world. As you read these selections, try to imagine how they would sound if spoken aloud.

Buffalo hide painted with images from Kiowa stories. In the center is the figure of saynday, the spirit in human form. The Kiowa believed that saynday created the world.

4

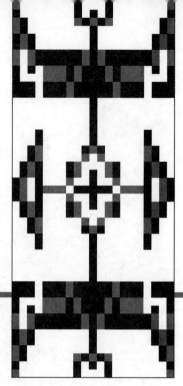

INTRODUCTION
The First Cure

The following selection is from a book called *Black Elk Speaks*. The book presents the spiritual values that Black Elk, an Oglala medicine man, experiences in a vision during his nation's troubled times in the mid-1800s. Black Elk believed that his purpose in life was to "save his great vision" for people of all groups, cultures, and places. Black Elk's story, spoken in Lakota and translated into English by his son, is a series of flashbacks and memories, rather than an organized account of his life and vision. It took the friendship and insight of John G. Neihardt, a poet familiar with Native American culture, to capture the spirituality of Black Elk's message.

The excerpt you are about to read describes one of Black Elk's visions that led him to an herb with healing power. His methods and cures were rooted in the traditional Oglala belief in nature as the giver of life and the Sun, Moon, and Winds as the "controllers" of the universe.

The First Cure
from *Black Elk Speaks*

as told through John G. Neihardt

. . . It was in the Moon of Shedding Ponies (May) when we had the heyoka ceremony.[1] One day in the Moon of Fatness (June), when everything was blooming, I invited One Side to come over and eat with me. I had been thinking about the four-rayed herb that I had now seen twice—the first time in the great vision[2] when I was nine years old, and the second time when I was lamenting[3] on the hill. I knew that I must have this herb for curing, and I thought I could recognize the place where I had seen it growing that night when I lamented.

After One Side and I had eaten, I told him there was a herb I must find, and I wanted him to help me hunt for it. Of course I did not tell him I had seen it in a vision. He was willing to help, so we got on our horses and rode over to Grass Creek. Nobody was living over there. We came to the top of a high hill above the creek, and there we got off our horses and sat down, for I felt that we were close to where I saw the herb growing in my vision of the dog.

---

1. **heyoka ceremony** (hay-YOH-kah SER-uh-moh-nee) *n.* a religious rite meant to show both serious and comic sides of life
2. **great vision** *n.* refers to a spiritual experience
3. **lamenting** (lah-MENT-ihng) *v.* to feel or express deep sorrow

We sat there awhile singing together some heyoka songs. Then I began to sing alone a song I had heard in my first great vision:

"In a sacred manner they are sending voices."

After I had sung this song, I looked down towards the west, and yonder at a certain spot beside the creek were crows and magpies, chicken hawks and spotted eagles circling around and around.

Then I knew, and I said to One Side: "Friend, right there is where the herb is growing." He said: "We will go forth and see." So we got on our horses and rode down Grass Creek until we came to a dry gulch, and this we followed up. As we neared the spot the birds all flew away, and it was a place where four or five dry gulches came together. There right on the side of the bank the herb was growing, and I knew it, although I had never seen one like it before, except in my vision.

It had a root about as long as to my elbow, and this was a little thicker than my thumb. It was flowering in four colors, blue, white, red, and yellow.

We got off our horses, and after I had offered red willow bark to the Six Powers, I made a prayer to the herb, and said to it: "Now we shall go forth to the two-leggeds, but only to the weakest ones, and there shall be happy days among the weak."

It was easy to dig the herb, because it was growing in the edge of the clay gulch. Then we started back with it. When we came to Grass Creek again, we wrapped it in some good sage that was growing there.

Something must have told me to find the herb just then, for the next evening I needed it and could have done nothing without it.

I was eating supper when a man by the name of Cuts-to-Pieces came in, and he was saying: "Hey, hey, hey!" for he was in trouble. I asked him what was the matter, and he said: "I have a boy of mine, and he is very sick and I am afraid he will die soon. He has been sick a long time. They say you have great power from the horse dance and the heyoka ceremony, so maybe you can save him for me. I think so much of him."

I told Cuts-to-Pieces that if he really wanted help, he should go home and bring me back a pipe with an eagle feather on it. While he was gone, I thought about what I had to do; and I was afraid, because I had never cured anybody yet with my power, and I was very sorry for Cuts-to-Pieces. I prayed hard for help. When Cuts-to-Pieces came back with the pipe, I told him to take it around to the left of me, leave it there, and pass out again to the right of me. When he had done this, I sent for One Side to come and help me. Then I took the pipe and went to where the sick little boy was. My father and my mother went with us, and my friend, Standing Bear, was already there.

I first offered the pipe to the Six Powers, then I passed it, and we all smoked. After that I began making a rumbling thunder sound on the drum. You know, when the power of the west comes to the two-leggeds, it comes with rumbling, and when it has passed, everything lifts up its head and is glad and there is greenness. So I made this rumbling sound. Also, the voice of the drum is an offering to the Spirit of the World. Its sound arouses the mind and makes men feel the mystery and power of things.

The sick little boy was on the northeast side of the tepee,[4] and when we entered at the south, we went around from left to right, stopping on the west side when we had made the circle.

---

4. **tepee** (TEE-pee) *n.* a cone-shaped tent made of animal skins

You want to know why we always go from left to right like that. I can tell you something of the reason, but not all. Think of this: Is not the south the source of life, and does not the flowering stick truly come from there? And does not man advance from there toward the setting sun of his life? Then does he not approach the colder north where the white hairs are? And does he not then arrive, if he lives, at the source of light and understanding, which is the east? Then does he not return to where he began, to his second childhood, there to give back his life to all life, and his flesh to the earth whence it came? The more you think about this, the more meaning you will see in it.

As I said, we went into the tepee from left to right, and sat ourselves down on the west side. The sick little boy was on the northeast side, and he looked as though he were only skin and bones. I had the pipe, the drum and the four-rayed herb already, so I asked for a wooden cup, full of water, and an eagle bone whistle, which was for the spotted eagle of my great vision. They placed the cup of water in front of me; and then I had to think awhile, because I had never done this before and I was in doubt.

I understood a little more now, so I gave the eagle bone whistle to One Side and told him how to use it in helping me. Then I filled the pipe with red willow bark, and gave it to the pretty young daughter of Cuts-to-Pieces, telling her to hold it, just as I had seen the virgin of the east holding it in my great vision.

Everything was ready now, so I made low thunder on the drum, keeping time as I sent forth a voice. Four times I cried "Hey-a-a-hey," drumming as I cried to the Spirit of the World, and while I was doing this I could feel the power coming through me from my feet up, and I knew that I could help the sick little boy.

I kept on sending a voice, while I made low thunder on the drum, saying: "My Grandfather, Great Spirit, you are the only one and to no other can anyone send voices. You have made everything, they say, and you have made it good and beautiful. The four quarters and the two roads crossing each other, you have made. Also you have set a power where the sun goes down. The two-leggeds on earth are in despair. For them, my Grandfather, I send a voice to you. You have said this to me: The weak shall walk. In vision you have taken me to the center of the world and there you have shown me the power to make over. The water in the cup that you have given me, by its power shall the dying live. The herb that you have shown me, through its power shall the feeble walk upright. From where we are always facing (the south), behold, a virgin shall appear, walking the good red road, offering the pipe as she walks, and hers also is the power of the flowering tree. From where the Giant lives (the north), you have given me a sacred, cleansing wind, and where this wind passes the weak shall have strength. You have said this to me. To you and to all your powers and to Mother Earth I send a voice for help."

You see, I had never done this before, and I know now that only one power would have been enough. But I was so eager to help the sick little boy that I called on every power there is.

I had been facing the west, of course, while sending a voice. Now I walked to the north and to the east and to the south, stopping there where the source of all life is and where the good red road begins. Standing there, I sang thus:

"In a sacred manner I have made them walk.
A sacred nation lies low.
In a sacred manner I have made them walk.
A sacred two-legged, he lies low.
In a sacred manner, he shall walk."

While I was singing this I could feel something queer all through my body, something that made me want to cry for all unhappy things, and there were tears on my face.

Now I walked to the quarter of the west, where I lit the pipe, offered it to the powers, and, after I had taken a whiff of smoke, I passed it around.

When I looked at the sick little boy again, he smiled at me, and I could feel that the power was getting stronger.

I next took the cup of water, drank a little of it, and went around to where the sick little boy was. Standing before him, I stamped the earth four times. Then, putting my mouth to the pit of his stomach, I drew through him the cleansing wind of the north. I next chewed some of the herb and put it in the water, afterward blowing some of it on the boy and to the four quarters. The cup with the rest of the water I gave to the virgin, who gave it to the sick little boy to drink. Then I told the virgin to help the boy stand up and to walk around the circle with him, beginning at the south, the source of life. He was very poor and weak, but with the virgin's help he did this.

Then I went away.

Next day Cuts-to-Pieces came and told me that his little boy was feeling better and was sitting up and could eat something again. In four days he could walk around. He got well and lived to be thirty years old.

Cuts-to-Pieces gave me a good horse for doing this; but of course I would have done it for nothing.

When the people heard about how the little boy was cured, many came to me for help, and I was busy most of the time.

This was in the summer of my nineteenth year (1882), in the Moon of Making Fat.

AFTER YOU READ

Exchanging Backgrounds and Cultures

1. What role does the sound of the drum play in Black Elk's ability to heal?

2. How do Black Elk's methods for healing reflect the Oglala belief in the power of nature?

3. What does Black Elk's statement, "I would have done it for nothing," reveal about his values?

What Do You Think?

Which character, event, or image in this story was most meaningful to you? Why was it special?

Experiencing Oral Tradition

In this account, Black Elk describes how he helped his people by finding the herb he saw in his vision. Think of an incident from your own life in which you helped someone. Then tell the story of this experience to a classmate as though it were an oral tradition.

Optional Activity   Remember that in oral tradition, words and images are often repeated to make stories more memorable. Throughout his account, Black Elk repeated certain images, such as the rumbling sound of the drum. Write a brief descriptive passage about an aspect of nature. Be sure to repeat words and images.

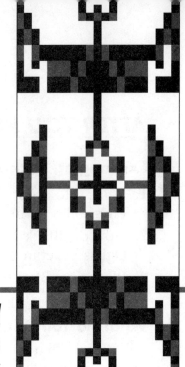

INTRODUCTION

from Madonna Swan: A Lakota Woman's Story

The following excerpt is from the book *Madonna Swan: A Lakota Woman's Story.* The book is a collection of stories about Madonna Swan's experiences on a reservation in South Dakota. Based on conversations and interviews Madonna Swan had with Mark St. Pierre, a scholar of Native American culture, the stories reveal the beliefs and values of the Lakota culture. For instance, the Lakota placed great value on the firstborn male and female children. As the firstborn female, Madonna Swan held a special place in her large family. She learned to believe in the virtues that govern the conduct of the Lakota people, such as generosity, bravery, courage, and honesty, through her parents and grandparents.

The stories that follow describe Madonna Swan's early childhood and the hardships of growing up on the Plains in the 1930s. Through these stories, Madonna Swan introduces us to her family, including her grandfather, Grandpa Puts On His Shoes, who was born long before there were reservations.

from *Madonna Swan:*
A Lakota Woman's Story

as told through Mark St. Pierre

I, MADONNA MARY SWAN ABDALLA, was born to the union of James Hart Swan and Lucy Josephine High Pine-Swan, September 12, 1928. I was the fifth child of the ten children born to this family. Only five of the ten children survived until adulthood. Manuel, the oldest, was born in 1919. He was a healthy baby, and one year after his birth, Mom had a big giveaway[1] to honor her firstborn. She gave away a tipi,[2] beaded cradleboards,[3] saddlebags, horses, Pendleton blankets, and many quilts. She gave away everything she had been given to start her married life.

Shirley Suzzana was born in 1921 but died of pneumonia later that same year. Kermit Joseph was born in 1924 and died of a wound received during World War II.

Austin Paul was born in 1926 and died of a head

---

1. **giveaway** *n.* a common social ritual; this particular one takes place at Thanksgiving
2. **tipi** (TEE-pee) *n.* the same as teepee, a cone-shaped tent made of animal skins
3. **cradleboards** (KRAY-duhl-bawrdz) *n.* devices for carrying a baby on a person's back, like a backpack

injury at four years old. He fell off a bed at Grandmother High Pine's place on the White River. Austin got sick after the fall, and his stomach got bigger and bigger. Mom and Grandma tried to give him an enema, but he got worse. By the time they got him to the hospital in Rosebud, it was too late. He died later that night.

Shirley Monica was born in 1930. Orby was born in 1932 and died as a teenager. He suffered from cerebral palsy, but he was a very bright boy and very close to Mom. Martha Mary was born in 1934 and died the next day. The last female child born to my parents was Ivy Lucy, born in 1942. She died in infancy. Erskin Elias, my mother's last child, was born in 1944, and he still lives in Cherry Creek.

From the children that died, it might seem that we had it very bad, but we didn't. We were born to a very strong mother whose love and patience more than made up for everything we went without. My dad finished high school at Chilocco[4] Indian School and took two years postgraduate work at Lawrence, Kansas. He had more education than any man of his generation and always stressed the importance of using our minds. Dad had his problems, but he always seemed to provide for us in the way of food, clothes, and school supplies.

Grandpa Puts On His Shoes

MY EARLIEST memories were of those years we lived in Iron Lightning community, with my grandfather, Puts On His Shoes. His land was north of the trading post at Red Elm, South Dakota. The government had built him a frame house when the reservation was settled many years earlier. They called these little frame houses "chief's houses" because they had been built for important men.

---

4. **Chilocco** (shi-LOH-koh) *n.* Indian school still operating in Oregon, featuring agricultural studies

The frame house had a kitchen, a bedroom, and a large room upstairs. That is where my father and mother, my brothers Kermit and Manuel, my sister Shirley, and I lived. We all lived with my grandfather and were happy there. . . .

Grandpa Puts, we called him, was alone then. His wife had passed away many years earlier, and he had no children still living. So he drank quite a bit, but he never got into trouble. He never fought anyone or was put in jail. Usually, he was a kind and wise man, a good grandfather. He lived a long life.

I don't know when he was born, but it was before there were the reservations. He was an old warrior, an old-fashioned Indian, what the white people called a chief. Grandpa Puts told us many stories of the old times when the Lakota people were free.

Memories of Old-Timers

WHEN I WAS a little girl, many of the old people who had lived before the reservations were still among us. They were different from people living now. They were stately people who carried themselves and spoke with respect all the time, even to white people. My grandfather was one of those old-timers. He told us many times, "Never trust a white man," but he didn't dislike all white people and had friends who were white. They spoke with him in Indian because he spoke no English.

Grandpa was a thin man and always wore a chief's blanket, its wide beaded strip around his middle. His hair was black mixed with silver and was always wrapped with rags or wool strips. He wore white man's pants but never owned a pair of shoes; he always wore moccasins.

One day Grandfather took us for a long walk. We gathered parts of different plants. As we went along, Grandfather explained how they were used. When we got back to the house, Grandpa took some of the leaves and boiled them like tea. Then he washed his hair with this and told us if we did this, our hair would always be thick and black like his. Grandpa showed us how to gather red willow and strip and chop it up to make tobacco mixings. He had no white man's education but was a very wise man.

Grandpa never went to Christian church. He always prayed with his pipe and took sweat baths.[6] I never knew what that little hut that stood off from the main house was for. I was very young then and just starting to remember and understand the things that I saw and the things people told me.

One day these two old men, Lone Eagle and Jake Bull Eagle, came to sweat with Grandpa Puts On His Shoes. Soon another old man named Swift Bear joined them. They visited and drank coffee. Late in the afternoon they headed down the hill towards a flat place where the sweat lodge stood. The old men gathered wood and stones and covered the sweat lodge with an old buffalo robe and quilts.

I asked Mom, "What are those men going to do?"

She replied, "They are going to take a sweat bath. One of those men has not been feeling well, and they are going to pray to the Grandfathers[6] to find out what is wrong with him."

"When are they going to do that?" I asked.

"Probably this evening at dusk," she said, and went on peeling and braiding the wild turnips she had dug that morning. . . .

Later that summer, I remember, Mom pitched Chief William White Swan's tipi. White Swan was my dad's father; he died long before I was born. White Swan was

---

5. **sweat baths** (SWET BATHS) *n.* purification rituals
6. **the Grandfathers** *n.* the spirits of sacred animals or ancestors who might help someone

Grandpa Puts's brother. Puts used to put that tipi up every summer. I guess he did it to remember and honor his brother. The tipi was made of buffalo hide and was a chief's tipi, so the smoke flaps were painted black. On either side of the door were painted figures of horses and buffalos. Inside, Grandpa placed some old buffalo robes and willow back rests. He stayed in there for about a month. When visitors came, they would go in there and smoke and visit with Grandpa. They spoke a lot of the old days, but I never remember them talking about battles.

Sometimes the old men would get into a heated debate about one thing or another, yet always they were friendly when it was over. They said things to each other in harsh words; still, they never swore. They seemed to understand that it takes discussion and argument to make decisions or get along. Today the slightest disagreement, and some people will pout for weeks or even months. People think that to argue or debate is not Indian. That is not true.

Dust Bowl

IN 1933 very little rain came. It had been this way for quite a while, I think. The ground was bone dry, and the berry bushes produced nothing that year. Sometimes great clouds of dust would blow, and the sky would get dark. Grandfather Puts On His Shoes said this was very bad and that a sun dance should be held to break the drought. I've heard that sun dances were held on other reservations to break the very bad weather.

The drought affected everyone, white and Indian alike. One day my grandfather took us to the town of Faith, South Dakota. When we got to town, we noticed a large crowd gathered on the south side of town, out on the prairie. We went over there, and here a great big hole had been dug. There were a lot of men and cattle near the hole. They were shooting their cattle and throwing the cattle into the hole. Grandpa went to ask one of his white friends why they were doing this. "There is no feed or water. The cattle are starving to death. We can't stand to see them suffer any more," the white man spoke in Indian. "You and your family can butcher as many as you want. They are not diseased, just starving."

We camped north of the railroad depot. Soon Dad came with the other wagon. Grandpa walked over to the wagon and said, "Nephew, these white men are killing their herds because there is no more feed or water around here. They said we could butcher as many as we want." My dad was kind of funny about certain things. If someone brought a deer or an antelope to the house to give us, he wouldn't eat it. My dad believed that deer were put on the earth for the sake of beauty, not to be eaten. So anyway, Grandpa kept telling Dad to go over and get some meat. "I'll even butcher it for you," Grandpa said, but Dad didn't want any.

Other families, like the Knifes and Lone Eagles, were there, and they were butchering, so they gave Mom some big pieces of meat to jerk. We got some meat anyway, and Grandpa got some soup. The Knifes are related to us through Grandpa Puts On His Shoes's family.

Leaving Iron Lightning and Grandpa

LATE IN THE summer of 1933 my father had decided to move back to his home community of Cherry Creek. Because Puts On His Shoes was my father's uncle, brother to White Swan, in the Indian way he was my dad's father also. Grandpa did not want us to move. He told my father that if he stayed he could have the land and the house for his own and whichever of the horses he wanted. Still, Dad was determined to leave. We hated to go; we loved Grandpa Puts. He had always been kind and gentle towards us, bringing candy and telling us stories.

When Dad told Grandpa we were leaving for sure, Grandpa was very sad, but he was a true man. He said, "If you wish to leave and your mind cannot be changed, then I'll give you a wagon and some horses for the trip. I have no son, and when I leave this earth, this land and house will be yours also." He must have given my dad and brothers twenty horses all together. Among them were mares, geldings, saddle horses, and a team and wagon. He gave these to us,[7] so we had two wagons, an old one and the new one Grandpa had given us.

When the day came, Mom and Dad loaded the wagons. It was a hot day late in August. Grandpa said, "Make sure you leave room for my brother White Swan's tipi. I am afraid if something should happen to me, no one would care for it. I am too old to put it up anymore."

Dad said, "We don't have room for it. I will come back after it." So we left it, and that was the last we saw of White Swan's tipi.

When we were in the wagons, ready to leave, Grandfather shook our hands, then he took our hands in his, and holding us like that he said, "Be brave and always pray every day to Wakon Tonka, because he is our great helper and will be throughout your life." He went on to say, "Never trust a white man behind your back! They will stab you, in one way or another!"

Grandfather had been through the wars and the troubles and knew what he was talking about. We were ready to leave, so Kermit and Manuel saddled two ponies and started to run the other horses ahead of us. We said our last goodbyes and started on our journey to Cherry Creek. Mom drove one team and wagon, my dad the other.

---

7. **He gave these to us** Grandpa Puts On His Shoes displays a Lakota value by handling his sorrow quietly. He also shows generosity by giving presents without expecting anything in return.

We traveled three days, first camping at Faith overnight. Early the next day the wagons started out again. That night our family camped in Red Scaffold. We stayed there overnight, then started out across the prairie the next morning, towards my Uncle Frank Council Bear's home. He lived on Bull Creek, west of Cherry Creek. We stopped to rest and fix lunch near Felix Creek a few miles from my uncle's place. Mom was going to start a fire and make tea and coffee. We had our lunch with us, boiled eggs, potatoes, and bread. Our plan was to eat quickly and get moving again.

The boys ate first because Dad told them, "Go ahead and eat; then drive the horses to Uncle Frank's place and wait for us there." It was a very windy day, so we rode down into a draw, a sheltered place out of the wind. Mom built a fire and made coffee and tea, and here, that fire got away! It started burning the dry grass. We had started a prairie fire! My father took both of the wagons across the creek and put them on the north side with us smaller kids inside. Next, he moved all of the horses over there also. Mom, Dad, and my two brothers began to fight the fire with spades and shovels, using them to swat the fire and dig a fire break. They moved in a circle around the fire, yet by the time they put it out, it must have burned at least five acres! It was late in the afternoon when they got the fire out and we finally ate our lunch.

We finished lunch and started our journey again. That evening we got to my uncle's place, down on Bull Creek near the Cheyenne River. Uncle Frank was very glad to see us and said we should stay with them.

Killing the Wolf

WE LIKED LIVING with our aunt and uncle on Bull Creek. There were more women to help with the house chores, so we got to spend more time with Mom. She liked to go out and sit in the evenings after supper. We girls would sometimes follow her. Mom would relax and turn her face towards the sun. She looked so pretty like that. Us kids would beg her to tell us a story. She would tease us back, saying, "No, you don't want to hear one of those old stories again, do you?"

"Sure we do."

"Well, okay then," and she started.

"When I was eight or nine years old, and my little brother Thomas was four, my brothers Henry and George were also there. We lived in a tent.[8] It was a big wall tent, so inside was a cook stove and wood heater. The tent had a liner to keep us warm. My mother and father and the baby slept in a double bed in the northeast corner. That's where Mom slept even on nights when Dad was not home, like that night. Right next to theirs was my bed, standing east to west. On the other end of the tent there was another bed, and that was where my two brothers were sleeping.

"We were all asleep, but my mother, your grandmother, thought she heard something. She was listening, and here, something was eating real loud. In the dim moonlight, there was a wolf in our tent! She reached her hand over to me and woke me up. She told me, 'Something is eating at the stove, and I'm going to kill it. Grab your little brother here and wake Tom and George. All of you sit on the boys' bed.' Then she gave me a big piece of rawhide for a shield and waited for us to move. I was really scared. Mom picked up another piece of rawhide, for a shield, and an axe. When we were all ready, we sat there hardly breathing.

"That animal must have been really hungry, because it didn't even hear all this going on. Mom moved very slowly and went around behind it, then hit it very hard on the head. There was a loud yelp! That was all. It just fell over

---

8. **We lived in a tent.** Rectangular wall tents replaced the tipi during the summer; in the prairie tall pines for tipi poles were scarce.

dead. Mom told me to light a lamp, and here, she had killed a great big wolf! We all looked at it. Then Mom drug it by the tail, and she dropped it a little ways from our tent.

"The next morning I got up, got dressed, went out, and there it was, still lying there, so I called my brothers to come see it. My brother George looked at it and said he was going to ride into White River and tell the storekeeper. So he rode over there and told him about it. He was the only white man who lived near us then. The storekeeper went to Rosebud and told the farm agent to come look at it. The farm agent came over and took a picture of Grandma with the wolf. The picture was in the Episcopal newsletter called *Anpo Win* (Dawn Woman)!"

Grandma High Pine was visiting us that summer, and she had been sitting there listening quietly, smiling to herself.

"Is it true, Grandma? Did you kill that wolf?" Manuel asked.

"Sure, it's true! That wolf was old and deaf like I am now," she said. We laughed and laughed. Finally, Grandma couldn't hold it in any more, and she laughed with us. . . .

Moving to Cherry Creek

MY FATHER worked . . . in Bridger, but he had bought a house near Cherry Creek and had an addition built on it, so it was a big house. That was where we moved in the fall of 1934, so our journey was done.

Because we were living out in the country then, my brothers were my first real playmates. A little later that fall my cousin Mary Council Bear moved near us, so I sometimes got to play with her, and enjoyed that very much. We had some white neighbors that lived out in the country near us. They would come and play with us, too. They usually brought milk and eggs with them. Their mom would always send a note for our mom, asking her to send a prairie chicken or cottontail in return for the eggs. This made it nice for us, because we needed the milk and eggs, and my brothers were always hunting for something!

It seemed Mom always had a good garden. She watered it by hauling many loads of water up from the river. Mom would hitch the team and wagon, then haul large tins and barrels. While Mom was filling her containers, we would play along the river. Our favorite was to pick up round flat rocks, looking for just the right one to skip or throw at fish or whatever we liked. Shirley and I played all sorts of things on these trips, mostly using our imaginations. I don't remember having candy, but we would make Kool-Aid and drink nectar or pop in those days. For a treat Mom would make us cookies or popcorn. These were the only kinds of treats we had back then.

Sundays were always a happy and interesting day for me. Dad would take time to talk to us on Sundays or other family occasions. He would read the Bible, and Grandma High Pine would pray with her pipe. Dad would often pick out a scripture and relate it to our modern situation. He would use these times to teach us a lesson about people or life.

Even at an early age we were responsible for certain chores. We brushed our hair, braided it, and helped make breakfast with Mom or Grandma. Mom told us early in life how to do the dishes, not to let the food harden on the plates or they would be much harder to wash.

We all lived in one big room in the log house. Grandma had her own little cabin. We'd stop in and visit her on the way back from feeding the chickens. Later in the day we would make our beds. Often we would haul the bedding outdoors to air them out. Unlike some folks, we all had our own bed and headboards.

There was a time when we all learned to make our own mattresses. The wool came in big, tight gunny sacks. They were stuffed really hard, and it was hard for our small hands to pull the gray dusty wool from the sacks. The dust from the wool was giving us sore throats so Kermit tied handkerchiefs around our mouths and noses. That really helped a lot. After we pulled it out, we washed and dried it, then stuffed the mattresses.

It seemed that in those days we did most things for ourselves. Our best dresses were all handmade from calico, our play dresses from cotton flour sacking. Although we had little, it did not seem we wanted for much, and it often seemed as if we had it better than many other people around us; we were happy then. . . .

Lucy Marries

EVEN AFTER WHAT Mom told me about school, I was still afraid to be going so far from home; I didn't want Mom to be sad. I asked her, "How did you meet Dad? At school?"

"Yes, it was at school, but your dad was not a student. He had already finished school long before that. He had moved back to the reservation and married a woman named Mattie High Dog. She died, so your father was at home alone.

"One of my friends sent a letter that spring to a male cousin of hers. She told him she had found the perfect wife for him. She told me that she had the perfect husband for me. She said, His name is James Hart Swan. He has been to school in Chilocco, Oklahoma, and he even has two years past high school at Lawrence, Kansas. He is very educated and very handsome and comes from a good family. His father was a chief.

"One day my friend ran over to where I was working. 'He's coming! He's coming!' she yelled.

'Who?' I asked.

'My cousin, James. He's coming to meet you. If you're right for him, he wants to marry you!' 'Marry me! Oh, no, I thought. I'm just a little girl!'

"Why, just last summer I spent most of my time riding from powwow to powwow on the reservation with my sister, I told her. Oh, what fun we had, though. We stayed with older relatives. Whenever we needed money, I took a tooth off the elk's tooth dress Mom let me use. I would sell the tooth and then we would have money. It still makes me laugh. Donna, when I think about how angry your Grandma got when she saw the dress!

"Still I told my friend, 'I am too young; this man will never want to marry me.'

"Well, he came, and he was handsome, and so old, I thought. He asked me if I could sew. 'Yes,' I said.

'Can you cook?'

'Yes, I can.'

'Do you know how to hitch a team?'

'Yes. I can do beadwork, and make moccasins, and . . .'

'Never mind all that!' he said. 'If you marry me, you won't have to worry about any of that!'

'But I'm just so dumb. I'm only a sixth grader,' I told him.

'That's okay. You don't have to be educated; if you can read and figure and speak English, that's plenty,' he said.

"Soon he left. I never heard from him until I got a letter from my brother. He said James had gone to Rosebud, to White River, and spoke to him about me. In the letter he said, 'This man has no wife; he has gone to high school, and even beyond that! He seems like a good man, and I am sure he can take care of you.'

"Mom didn't like the idea at all. Still, my brother was the man of the family, now that my dad was gone, and he said to marry this man. My friend helped me make a wedding dress, and many presents for me, even for a baby! They teased me so much; we would just laugh, imagining what it would be like to be married. About two weeks after the letter came, James came to the school with my brother George, and we drove to White River. We were married there, stayed a few days with my mother, then moved to Cherry Creek.

"So you see, I was young, too young. I want you to go to Immaculate Conception Mission and learn all you can. I want you to finish high school and be a nurse or something that you want—something so you could make your own way in this world with your brains and education. That is what your father wants for you also. I know when you leave for school you will be lonely; so will I. We will all miss you very much, but we will have the summers together, and we will visit you as often as we can. So when you go to school, pay attention, learn all you can."

I didn't really feel any better about leaving home, but if this was what Mom and Dad both wanted, I thought, "I will go along with it and try not to be sad.". . .

Robert Blue Hair's Mother

THE SIOUX HAVE many medicine people who use herbs, songs, and the pipe to doctor the sick. My grandfathers, Thin Elk and Runs Above, were medicine men like this. They cured sicknesses and helped many people.

When I was eight years old, we went to the Fourth of July in Faith. My dad was going to take us to the rodeo—a real rodeo! We were all excited, but that time I had a real bad tooth ache, and I was really suffering with it. Dad had a car then, and I was lying in the back seat.

I was too sick to go to the rodeo, and I was disappointed. I just cried. There was a woman from Cherry Creek who was a good herb doctor. Her name was Mrs. Blue Hair, and she was a real old-fashioned Indian woman. Mom saw Mrs. Blue Hair and her family camped not too far from us at the Faith fair. Mom went to talk to Mrs. Blue Hair about my toothache. "Yes, I can help her, at least until she has it pulled or fixed. Lay her down on the cot in your wall tent then pull the flaps down. I'll be over in a minute."

Soon Mom told me to get in the tent and pull the flaps down. "Why? What for? I asked.

"She is going to try and doctor that tooth so you can go the rodeo," Mom said. Mrs. Blue Hair came. First she sang and prayed in Indian with her hands outstretched to each direction. When she had finished the medicine song, she bent over me. She sounded like a bear was in her chest. Mrs. Blue Hair took some white powdered medicine from a little buckskin sack and rubbed it all over my tooth. It looked like chalk. When she was finished, it hurt less. By the time the rodeo was ready to begin, my tooth was much better. . . .

Horse Grandchildren

DAD WAS NOT home much of the time. It is a good thing that Mom was an independent and resourceful person. Grandma and Grandpa High Pine had done a good job with Mom, preparing her for motherhood and life.

I remember early one summer, when I was about ten, it was 1938. An elderly person Mom thought highly of had passed away. She was being waked in a small church about twenty-five miles from Cherry Creek. Mom wanted to pay her last respects and help with the butchering and cooking for the feast that always follows the funeral and burial. It had rained for two days, and puddles stood everywhere on the gumbo. Mom said, "It will be muddy! I hope we don't get stuck. We'll take the best team and the newer wagon that Grandpa gave us.

"Madonna, go tell Ida One Feather to gather her kids and anything she wants to bring, so we can pack the wagon box." So I did. I ran all the way. Mrs. One Feather was a friend of Mom's, and she had two boys and a little girl to take with her.

We were finished loading and hitching the team to the wagon about 11:00 in the morning. The sun had disappeared behind dark clouds, and it looked threatening. "Come, let's get started," Mom called out. There were six of us all together, and our clothes, tents, and cooking supplies, so the wagon was quite heavy. We made deep ruts in the soft clay as we started for the wake.

About six miles from Cherry Creek there was a low place near the Cheyenne River that looked muddy, even from a distance. We were only a few yards into that place when we got stuck. Cornelius One Feather, Ida's oldest boy, asked Mom, "Should I get out and give the horses a slap so we can get going again?" "No, I'll do it," Mom said.

Mom reached under the seat and took out some oats and some rags. We all watched. She was smiling and sort of laughing out loud as she tied the rags around her shoes. She climbed down off the wagon and sank in wet gumbo clay up to her ankles. She could barely move as she struggled to get nearer the horses. She gave each of the horses a handful of oats and stroked their heads. She said, "Takoja unsilakano unpi yapi omani le elunkiiyapi na aka ehunpi woaste un komanipi ca. (Grandsons, help us! Help us that we will get out of this swamp and mud and take us to safety to where we are going. We are going for a good purpose)." She didn't get angry; she talked to them like they were people.[9] She never got angry or cursed. She just spoke very gently to them and rubbed their faces. Mom gave a gentle tug, and the horses strained to pull the wagon. It budged with a jolt and started to move.

Every time we got stuck, Mom would climb down with her gumbo-covered feet and talk with the horses. It took a while, but finally we made higher, drier ground. Mom climbed down and thanked the horses. Then she put her hands on her hips and pretended to do a little dance. We all howled with laughter. Finally, Mom couldn't hold it back anymore, and she started laughing so hard she couldn't continue her dance. Those gumbo clods were about a foot thick, and they made her feet look huge.

Late that day we got to the church. Mom had taken us over a rough road with no man. That's the kind of Mom she was. Nothing seemed to scare her. She faced life head on, often by herself.

---

9. **she talked to them like they were people** It is a Lakota belief that each animal has a spirit and a form of intelligence for its kind.

AFTER YOU READ

Exchanging Backgrounds and Cultures

1. How does the character of Grandpa Puts On His Shoes give you insight into Lakota values and beliefs?
2. What role do those values and beliefs play in Grandpa Puts On His Shoes's attitude toward white people?
3. Why do you think he advises his grandchildren to "never trust a white man"?

What Do You Think?

Which part of the excerpt did you find especially interesting? What made it meaningful for you?

Experiencing Oral Tradition

In parts of this excerpt, Madonna Swan describes a few of her childhood memories and family traditions. Tell a story of a childhood memory that you recall, or a holiday tradition observed by your family. Include descriptions of the setting and people involved, and convey the reasons that the experience was memorable.

Optional Activity Think about someone that you know well and find interesting. Then write about an episode in this person's life that reveals qualities that you find worth imitating.

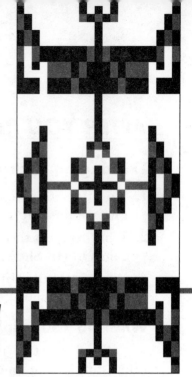

INTRODUCTION
Remaking the World

Traditional stories are passed down from generation to generation. They usually attempt to explain occurrences in nature or the origin of humanity. The stories of a certain culture often indirectly reflect its values and beliefs. The Lakota, like most Native American nations, believe that mysterious powers dwell in all aspects of nature, including animals, mountains, rivers, and rocks. Thriving with life, these natural elements are therefore connected to the world of human beings.

The following traditional story, "Remaking the World," is about the destruction and re-creation of the "Turtle Continent." As such, it reflects the Lakota belief in the power of nature and supernatural forces. The story was retold in 1974 on the Rosebud Indian Reservation by Leonard Crow Dog, a Brulé medicine man and descendant of Crow Dog, a famous chief and warrior. As you read, pay careful attention to the pattern Leonard Crow Dog creates through the repetition of certain words, images, and ideas.

Remaking the World
from *American Indian Myths and Legends*

as told by Leonard Crow Dog

There was a world before this world, but the people in it did not know how to behave themselves or how to act human. The creating power was not pleased with that earlier world. He said to himself: "I will make a new world." He had the pipe bag and the chief pipe, which he put on the pipe rack that he had made in the sacred manner. He took four dry buffalo chips, placed three of them under the three sticks, and saved the fourth one to light the pipe.

The Creating Power said to himself: "I will sing three songs, which will bring a heavy rain. Then I'll sing a fourth song and stamp four times on the earth, and the earth will crack wide open. Water will come out of the cracks and cover all the land." When he sang the first song, it started to rain. When he sang the second, it poured. When he sang the third, the rain-swollen rivers overflowed their beds. But when he sang the fourth song and stamped on the earth, it split open in many places like shattered gourd,[1] and water flowed from the cracks until it covered everything.

---

1. **gourd** (GAWRD) *n.* the dried, hollowed-out shell of a squash, melon, or cucumber used as a drinking cup, dipper, etc.

The Creating Power floated on the sacred pipe and on his huge pipe bag. He let himself be carried by waves and wind this way and that, drifting for a long time. At last the rain stopped, and by then all the people and animals had drowned. Only Kangi,[2] the crow, survived, though it had no place to rest and was very tired. Flying above the pipe, "Tunkashila,[3] Grandfather, I must soon rest"; and three times the crow asked him to make a place for it to light.

The Creating Power thought: "It's time to unwrap the pipe and open the pipe bag." The wrapping and the pipe bag contained all manner of animals and birds, from which he selected four animals known for their ability to stay under water for a long time. First he sang a song and took the loon[4] out of the bag. He commanded the loon to dive and bring up a lump of mud. The loon did dive, but it brought up nothing. "I dived and dived but couldn't reach bottom," the loon said. "I almost died. The water is too deep."

The Creating Power sang a second song and took the otter out of the bag. He ordered the otter to dive and bring up some mud. The sleek otter at once dived into the water, using its strong webbed feet to go down, down, down. It was submerged for a long time, but when it finally came to the surface, it brought nothing.

Taking the beaver out of the pipe's wrapping, the Creating Power sang a third song. He commanded the beaver to go down deep below the water and bring some mud. The beaver thrust itself into the water, using its great flat tail to propel itself downward. It stayed under water longer than the others, but when it finally came up again, it too brought nothing.

---

2. **Kangi** (KAHN-jee) *n.* word used by Lakota for Crow tribe
3. **Tunkashila** (TOONK-uh-shee-la) "Grandfather Spirit" of the Lakota
4. **loon** (LOON) *n.* a type of fishing-eating diving bird with a sharp bill, noted for its strange cry

At last the Creating Power sang the fourth song and took the turtle out of the bag. The turtle is very strong. Among our people it stands for long life and endurance and the power to survive. A turtle heart is great medicine, for it keeps on beating a long time after the turtle is dead. "You must bring the mud," the Creating Power told the turtle. It dove into the water and stayed below so long that the other three animals shouted: "The turtle is dead; it will never come up again!"

All the time, the crow was flying around and begging for a place to light.

After what seemed to be eons,[5] the turtle broke the surface of the water and paddled to the Creating Power. "I got to the bottom!" the turtle cried. "I brought some earth!" And sure enough, its feet and claws—even the space in the cracks on its sides between its upper and lower shell—were filled with mud.

Scooping mud from the turtle's feet and sides, the Creating Power began to sing. He sang all the while that he shaped the mud in his hands and spread it on the water to make a spot of dry land for himself. When he had sung the fourth song, there was enough land for the Creating Power and for the crow.

"Come down and rest," said the Creating Power to the crow, and the bird was glad to.

Then the Creating Power took from his bag two long wing feathers of the eagle. He waved them over his plot of ground and commanded it to spread until it covered everything. Soon all the water was replaced by earth. "Water without earth is not good," thought the Creating Power, "but land without water is not good either." Feeling pity for the land, he wept for the earth and the creatures he would put upon it, and his tears became oceans, streams, and lakes. "That's better," he thought.

---

5. eons (EE-uhnz) *n.* billions of years

Out of his pipe bag the Creating Power took all kinds of animals, birds, plants and scattered them over the land. When he stamped on the earth, they all came alive.

From the earth the Creating Power formed the shapes of men and women. He used red earth and white earth, black earth and yellow earth, and made as many as he thought would do for a start. He stamped on the earth and the shapes came alive, each taking the color of the earth out of which it was made. The Creating Power gave all of them understanding and speech and told them what tribes they belonged to.

The Creating Power said to them: "The first world I made was bad; the creatures on it were bad. So I burned it up. The second world I made was bad too, so I drowned it. This is the third world I have made. Look: I have created a rainbow for you as a sign that there will be no more Great Flood. Whenever you see a rainbow, you will know that it has stopped raining."

The Creating Power continued: "Now, if you have learned how to behave like human beings and how to live in peace with each other and with the other living things— the two-legged, the four-legged, the many-legged, the fliers, the no-legs, the green plants of this universe—then all will be well. But if you make this world bad and ugly, then I will destroy this world too. It's up to you."

The Creating Power gave the people the pipe. "Live by it," he said. He named this land the Turtle Continent because it was there that the turtle came up with the mud out of which the third world was made.

"Someday there might be a fourth world," the Creating Power thought. Then he rested.

—Told by Leonard Crow Dog at Grass Mountain, Rosebud Indian Reservation, 1974. Recorded by Richard Erdoes.

AFTER YOU READ

Exchanging Backgrounds and Cultures

1. Which important Lakota values and beliefs does the turtle represent?
2. How does this traditional story explain the differences among people?
3. How must the people of the new world behave in order to survive?

What Do You Think?

Which part of this selection was most meaningful to you? Explain why it was so special.

Experiencing Oral Tradition

"Remaking the World" is based on the idea that the world needs to be recreated. What would you do to improve the world? Make a list of your ideas. Then create a myth about this new world using the ideas from your list.

Optional Activity Think about such natural phenomena as earthquakes, volcanos, constellations, and the forming of mountains. What occurrence in nature have you often wondered about? Write a brief story that explains the reason for the occurrence. In order to make your story memorable, remember to repeat certain images, words, and ideas.

UNIT I: FOCUS ON WRITING

The literature that makes up Native American oral tradition was intended to be heard rather than read. However, in order to preserve the traditional beliefs and the personal narratives of their cultures, many Native Americans told their stories to ethnographers (eth-NAHG-ruh-fuhrz). These are people who record the stories with two main objectives: to remain true to the speaker's words, tone, and rhythm and to organize the information in a way that will be clear to the audience. For instance, John Neihardt was chosen by Black Elk to record and organize his great visions and flashbacks so that future generations could learn from them.

Writing a Personal Account

Choose a classmate that you would like to interview. The purpose of the interview is to learn about an interesting past experience in this person's life. After you have conducted the interview, retell the story in writing.

The Writing Process

Good writing requires both time and effort. An effective writer completes a number of stages that together make up the writing process. The stages of the writing process are given below to help guide you through your assignment.

Prewriting

The interview itself is part of the prewriting stage. Be sure to take notes as your classmate describes the experience. Rather than trying to copy down the story word for word, concentrate on the key points your classmate makes and any recurring images and phrases.

Before you begin to write out the account, take some time to consider your audience, purpose, and tone. Who will be reading this account? What aspect of the account do you want to focus on? Is it a happy, sad, scary, or funny story? What tone did the speaker use when relating it to you?

Next, review the notes that you took during the interview. Make a list of the vivid words and images your classmate used when describing the experience. Then arrange the details of the account in a logical order. Like Mark St. Pierre, who recorded the life experiences of Madonna Swan, you may find that chronological order—events arranged according to time—works best for a personal account.

Drafting and Revising

Once your prewriting is completed, you are ready to begin the drafting stage. A first draft is not supposed to be a perfect piece of writing. It is the process of getting down on paper the ideas you generated in the prewriting stage. Choose a drafting style that you feel comfortable with. Perhaps you like to draft quickly, getting the story down in very rough form and then going back to rework that draft considerably. Or you might prefer to draft more slowly and carefully, revising as you go along.

When revising the personal account, pay careful attention to the details, words, and images you used. Are the details accurate? Do the words and images capture the voice and tone of the speaker?

Proofreading and Publishing

After you have made the appropriate revisions, proofread the account for any errors in spelling, grammar, punctuation and capitalization. Try to allow some time between revising and proofreading. This will make it easier for you to notice any errors. Then make a final copy of your work.

Now your account is ready for an audience. Read it aloud to a discussion group, to the whole class, or to a different class. Then join your classmates in creating a publication that contains the accounts you all have written.

UNIT 2

NONFICTION OF THE PLAINS NATIVE AMERICANS

Writers of **nonfiction** present real people, real places, and actual events either past or present. There are many forms of nonfiction, ranging from formal government documents, such as laws and treaties, to very personal stories that unfold in autobiographies or biographies. Other forms of nonfiction include letters, diaries, journals, speeches, interviews, personal narratives, essays, and news articles. An important characteristic in all nonfiction is the inclusion of facts, or information that can be proven to be true. However, many writers of nonfiction combine facts with their personal thoughts, feelings, opinions, and values.

The personal aspect of nonfiction writing helps us to better understand different people, places, and times. The first selection, "The School Days of an Indian Girl," is an autobiographical sketch by Zitkala-Ša, a Yankton Lakota woman born in 1876. This sketch describes her earliest struggle to preserve her cultural heritage in a dominant society. "We've Got To Have Commitment So Strong. . . . ." is a speech by John Trudell, a Santee Lakota and spokesperson for the Native American civil rights movement of the 1960s and 1970s. In his speech, he calls for Native American unity and equality. As you read these selections, think about how these writers blend social and historical facts with their most private thoughts and opinions.

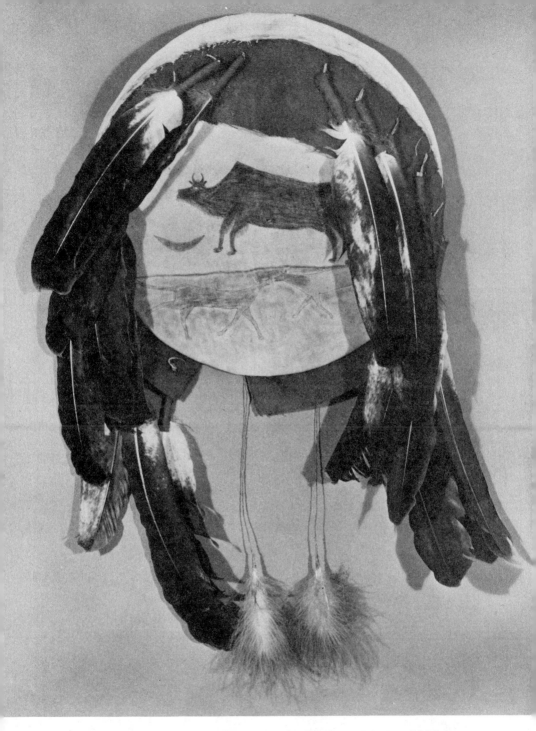

Comanche Shield. *State Museum, Oklahoma Historical Society,* Oklahoma City. Shield dates to the 1870s, and is made of hide, cotton fabric, wool, and eagle feathers, and painted with sacred images.

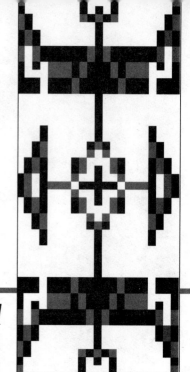

INTRODUCTION

The School Days of an Indian Girl

The 1800s marked a period of great change for many Native Americans, who found themselves denied their ancestral lands and confined to reservations because of the United States' expansion westward. Fearful that their oral traditions would disappear forever, some Native Americans began to write down the legends and folk tales of their nations, as well as their personal stories. Zitkala-Ša was one of the first Native Americans to preserve the cultural heritage of her nation in writing.

Born in 1876, Zitkala-Ša spent her early childhood on the Yankton reservation in South Dakota, where she was educated in the traditions of her culture. When she was eight years old, Zitkala-Ša left the reservation to study at White's Manual Institute, a missionary school in Indiana. Though White's was run by Quakers, it followed the Bureau of Indian Affairs' policy of adapting Native American children to white culture. The following excerpt, "The School Days of an Indian Girl," from Zitkala-Ša's autobiographical *American Indian Stories*, describes her earliest struggles with the conflict between tradition and change that would plague her for the rest of her life.

The School Days of an Indian Girl

from *American Indian Stories*

by Zitkala-Ša

I. THE LAND OF RED APPLES.

THERE were eight in our party of bronzed children who were going East with the missionaries.[1] Among us were three young braves, two tall girls, and we three little ones, Judéwin,[2] Thowin,[3] and I.

We had been very impatient to start on our journey to the Red Apple Country, which, we were told, lay a little beyond the great circular horizon of the Western prairie. Under a sky of rosy apples we dreamt of roaming as freely and happily as we had chased the cloud shadows on the Dakota plains. We had anticipated much pleasure from a ride on the iron horse,[4] but the throngs of staring palefaces disturbed and troubled us.

On the train, fair women, with tottering babies on each arm, stopped their haste and scrutinized[5] the children of absent mothers. Large men, with heavy

---

1. **missionaries** (MIHSH-uhn-air-eez) *n.* people sent to convert others to a particular religion
2. **Judéwin** (joo-DAY-wihn)
3. **Thowin** (THOH-wihn)
4. **iron horse** a train
5. **scrutinized** (SKROO-tih-neyezd) *n.* looked over carefully

bundles in their hands, halted near by, and riveted their glassy blue eyes upon us.

I sank deep into the corner of my seat, for I resented being watched. Directly in front of me, children who were no larger than I hung themselves upon the backs of their seats, with their bold white faces toward me. Sometimes they took their forefingers out of their mouths and pointed at my moccasined feet. Their mothers, instead of reproving such rude curiosity, looked closely at me, and attracted their children's further notice to my blanket. This embarrassed me, and kept me constantly on the verge of tears.

I sat perfectly still, with my eyes downcast, daring only now and then to shoot long glances around me. Chancing to turn to the window at my side, I was quite breathless upon seeing one familiar object. It was the telegraph pole which strode by at short paces. Very near my mother's dwelling, along the edge of a road thickly bordered with wild sunflowers, some poles like these had been planted by white men. Often I had stopped, on my way down the road, to hold my ear against the pole, and, hearing its low moaning, I used to wonder what the paleface had done to hurt it. Now I sat watching for each pole that glided by to be the last one.

In this way I had forgotten my uncomfortable surroundings, when I heard one of my comrades call out my name. I saw the missionary standing very near, tossing candies and gums into our midst. This amused us all, and we tried to see who could catch the most of the sweetmeats.

Though we rode several days inside of the iron horse, I do not recall a single thing about our luncheons.

It was night when we reached the school grounds. The lights from the windows of the large buildings fell upon some of the icicled trees that stood beneath them. We were led toward an open door, where the brightness of the lights within flooded out over the heads of the excited palefaces who blocked our way. My body trembled more from fear than from the snow I trod upon.

Entering the house, I stood close against the wall. The strong glaring light in the large whitewashed room dazzled my eyes. The noisy hurrying of hard shoes upon a bare wooden floor increased the whirring in my ears. My only safety seemed to be in keeping next to the wall. As I was wondering in which direction to escape from all this confusion, two warm hands grasped me firmly, and in the same moment I was tossed high in midair. A rosy-cheeked paleface woman caught me in her arms. I was both frightened and insulted by such trifling. I stared into her eyes, wishing her to let me stand on my own feet, but she jumped me up and down with increasing enthusiasm. My mother had never made a plaything of her wee daughter. Remembering this I began to cry aloud.

They misunderstood the cause of my tears, and placed me at a white table loaded with food. There our party were united again. As I did not hush my crying, one of the older ones whispered to me, "Wait until you are alone in the night."

It was very little I could swallow besides my sobs, that evening.

"Oh, I want my mother and my brother Dawée! I want to go to my aunt!" I pleaded; but the ears of the palefaces could not hear me.

From the table we were taken along an upward incline of wooden boxes, which I learned afterward to call a stairway. At the top was a quiet hall, dimly lighted. Many narrow beds were in one straight line down the entire length of the wall. In them lay sleeping brown faces, which peeped just out of the coverings. I was tucked into bed with one of the tall girls, because she talked to me in my mother tongue and seemed to soothe me.

I had arrived in the wonderful land of rosy skies, but I was not happy, as I had thought I should be. My long travel and the bewildering sights had exhausted me. I fell asleep, heaving deep, tired sobs. My tears were left to dry themselves in streaks, because neither my aunt nor my mother was near to wipe them away.

II. THE CUTTING OF MY LONG HAIR

The first day in the land of apples was a bitter-cold one; for the snow still covered the ground, and the trees were bare. A large bell rang for breakfast, its loud metallic voice crashing through the belfry overhead and into our sensitive ears. The annoying clatter of shoes on bare floors gave us no peace. The constant clash of harsh noises, with an undercurrent of many voices murmuring an unknown tongue, made a bedlam[6] within which I was securely tied. And though my spirit tore itself in struggling for its lost freedom, all was useless.

A paleface woman, with white hair, came up after us. We were placed in a line of girls who were marching into the dining room. These were Indian girls, in stiff shoes and closely clinging dresses. The small girls wore sleeved aprons and shingled[7] hair. As I walked noiselessly in my soft moccasins,[8] I felt like sinking to the floor, for my blanket had been stripped from my shoulders. I looked hard at the Indian girls, who seemed not to care that they were even more immodestly dressed than I, in their tightly fitting clothes. While we marched in, the boys entered at an opposite door. I watched for the three young braves[9] who came in our party. I spied them in the rear ranks, looking as uncomfortable as I felt.

A small bell was tapped, and each of the pupils drew a chair from under the table. Supposing this act meant they were to be seated, I pulled out mine and at once slipped

---

6. **bedlam** (BED-luhm) *n.* a noisy, confused scene
7. **shingled** (SHIHN-guhld) *adj.* cut short
8. **moccasins** (MAHK-uh-sihnz) *n.* slippers of soft leather worn by Native Americans
9. **braves** *n.* Native American warriors

into it from one side. But when I turned my head, I saw that I was the only one seated, and all the rest at our table remained standing. Just as I began to rise, looking shyly around to see how chairs were to be used, a second bell was sounded. All were seated at last, and I had to crawl back into my chair again. I heard a man's voice at one end of the hall, and I looked around to see him. But all the others hung their heads over their plates. As I glanced at the long chain of tables, I caught the eyes of a paleface woman upon me. Immediately I dropped my eyes, wondering why I was so keenly watched by the strange woman. The man ceased his mutterings, and then a third bell was tapped. Every one picked up his knife and fork and began eating. I began crying instead, for by this time I was afraid to venture anything more.

But this eating by formula was not the hardest trial in that first day. Late in the morning, my friend Judéwin gave me a terrible warning. Judéwin knew a few words of English; and she had overheard the paleface woman talk about cutting our long, heavy hair. Our mothers had taught us that only unskilled warriors who were captured had their hair shingled by the enemy. Among our people, short hair was worn by mourners, and shingled hair by cowards!

We discussed our fate some moments, and when Judéwin said, "We have to submit, because they are strong," I rebelled.

"No, I will not submit! I will struggle first!" I answered.

I watched my chance, and when no one noticed I disappeared. I crept up the stairs as quietly as I could in my squeaking shoes,—my moccasins had been exchanged for shoes. Along the hall I passed, without knowing whither I was going. Turning aside to an open door, I found a large room with three white beds in it. The windows were covered with dark green curtains, which made the room very dim. Thankful that no one was there, I directed my steps toward the corner farthest from the door. On my hands and knees I crawled under the bed, and cuddled myself in the dark corner.

From my hiding place I peered out, shuddering with fear whenever I heard footsteps near by. Though in the hall loud voices were calling my name, and I knew that even Judéwin was searching for me, I did not open my mouth to answer. Then the steps were quickened and the voices became excited. The sounds came nearer and nearer. Women and girls entered the room. I held my breath and watched them open closet doors and peep behind large trunks. Some one threw up the curtains, and the room was filled with sudden light. What caused them to stoop and look under the bed I do not know. I remember being dragged out, though I resisted by kicking and scratching wildly. In spite of myself, I was carried downstairs and tied fast in a chair.

I cried aloud, shaking my head all the while until I felt the cold blades of scissors against my neck, and heard them gnaw off one of my thick braids. Then I lost my spirit. Since the day I was taken from my mother I had suffered extreme indignities.[10] People had stared at me. I had been tossed about in the air like a wooden puppet. And now my long hair was shingled like a coward's! In my anguish I moaned for my mother, but no one came to comfort me. Not a soul reasoned quietly with me, as my own mother used to do; for now I was only one of many little animals driven by a herder.

---

10. **indignities** (ihn-DIHG-nuh-teez) *n.* things that humiliate, insult, or violate someone's dignity

AFTER YOU READ

Exchanging Backgrounds and Cultures

1. During her journey eastward, what does Zitkala-Ša reveal about her attitude toward white people?

2. How does Zitkala-Ša's refusal to have her hair cut reflect her traditional beliefs?

3. Why do you think the school insists that the Native American girls have their hair cut short?

What Do You Think?

Which image or situation in this excerpt did you find especially interesting? Why was it meaningful to you?

Experiencing Nonfiction

In this autobiographical sketch, Zitkala-Ša vividly describes her first trip away from home. What experiences would you choose to write about if you were preparing your own autobiography? For example, you may want to write about your first experience away from home or a trip that you have taken. Pick one situation that you think others would find most interesting. Then write an autobiographical sketch that relates the events in chronological order and includes descriptive details.

Optional Activity Remember that autobiographies are written from the author's perspective, and they often reveal the writer's attitudes, beliefs, and personality traits. For example, Zitkala-Ša expresses her attitude toward white people in "The School Days of an Indian Girl." Think about the type of impression you would want to make on readers if you were writing your autobiography. Write an autobiographical sketch where the event you describe reveals your personality and values.

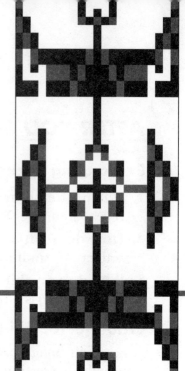

INTRODUCTION

We've Got to Have Commitment So Strong.....

John Trudell, a Santee Lakota born in 1945 in Omaha, Nebraska, experienced hardship from a very early age. Living in poverty on the Santee reservation, he watched his father struggle to provide for his large family. While serving in the Navy during the Vietnam War, Trudell saw the widespread racism in the U.S. military as a symptom of a biased and unjust society. In 1973, Trudell became the National Chairman of the American Indian Movement (AIM), a civil rights organization that seeks justice and equality for all Native Americans.

The following excerpt is from the speech Trudell delivered to other AIM members as they prepared for the International Treaty Conference in Geneva, Switzerland, in 1977. The speech focuses on the changes needed within AIM in order to improve the lives of the entire Native American community. As the title of the speech suggests, Trudell saw commitment, unity, and conviction among Native Americans as the only way to gain their freedom.

We've Got to Have Commitment So Strong. . . . .

by John Trudell

Before the International Treaty Conference of 1977 was held, members of the American Indian Movement (AIM) met in Cumberland, Wisconsin, to evaluate its course and to set priorities. There, the national chairman of AIM, John Trudell, spoke about changes that needed to take place within AIM in order for Native Americans to improve their lives. The following is an excerpt from his speech.

When we talk about discipline for the American Indian Movement, commitment is just about the number one thing to think about. . . .

We've got to have commitment so strong that we don't take no for an answer.

We've got to have commitment so strong that we will not accept their rhetoric[1] and lies for an answer.

We've got to have commitment so strong we will live and we will die for our people.

We've got to start thinking in terms of love. We get caught up in hating the white man for what he's done to us. And

---

1. rhetoric (RET-uhr-ihk) *n.* artificial, showy language

that hate shows; it shows internally in our own organization. We start playing the white men's games. We say we're out for the good of Indian people, but internally if we don't like what someone does, we start backstabbing. We start calling names; we start criticizing. We never come out in the open and talk to the individual or to the people we're displeased with and confront them with how we feel. We go around and agitate and try to build support amongst ourselves.

Sometimes I question—does the white man oppress us, or do we oppress ourselves?

. . . We have many complaints and many grievances against the white man and against the Bureau of Indian Affairs and against the state. We've got to understand things like colonialism. We've got to understand the process which the white man uses to exploit and keep us under his thumb.

Colonialism—that means that the white man came to our country and he took our land away from us and put us into reservations where he continues to exploit our resources and our lives. That's colonialism.

It's where we have white bosses and white landlords who come down to our communities and look good while we sit there hungry and sit there without our rights. That's colonialism.

Colonialism is when the Bureau of Indian Affairs is run by white people up in the Interior Department. And they get fat and they get rich and they keep us disoriented and they keep us at each other's throats. They keep us from gaining the working knowledge and the working experience we need to control our lives again. That's colonialism.

Our enemy is not the United States. Our enemy is not the individual white man. Our enemy is the collective white man. Our enemy is the American state. The American state is the corporations and the corrupt politicians that are selling us out. Those are the enemies.

The collective white man sits back and allows this to happen. He is our enemy. You know, when we're going to deal with the truth, the white man is going to have to accept this, because if there is ever going to be peace, love and understanding between the races, he's got to understand that he is in the wrong.

It was white people who created Capitalism. It was white people who created Communism. It was white people who created mission schools. It was white people who created jails. It was white people who robbed our land and it was white people who sat back in the corner and allowed their government to do it. And then they come to us and talk of love and brotherhood. . . .

They have no power—they have guns, they have bombs, they have their laws, they have methods and tools for destruction. But that is not power.

Power comes from the people.
Power comes from knowledge.
Power comes from love for the people.
Power comes from solidarity.
Power comes from not fighting each other.
Power comes from standing for the issues that we believe in.
Power comes from believing in our right to live. . . .

When Europeans first came here, we showed them how to live. We showed them how to survive. We gave them their economy, and they were peaceful to us. They were nice, because they did not know how to live here. Once they found out how to live here, then they started killing us. Then they started stealing our land. Then they brought the black man in to get him to farm and cultivate their land. Then they started their lies and their history of repression and oppression of the native indigenous people of this land.

Now they take us and pump us through their schools to listen to this and they tell us we are free. They say we live in a democracy. They tell us we've got human rights. And they get us to believe it.

They create the illusion of freedom because they create a civil rights bill that says you have certain rights. We know we have these rights. But why can't we send our kids to school with long hair? Why can't we put our people in to decide what our education is going to be? We cannot decide what our religion is going to be—we can't get our religion recognized.

There is no freedom in this country unless you are extremely rich—or unless you have liberated your own self. That's where freedom comes. . . .

AFTER YOU READ

Exchanging Backgrounds and Cultures

1. According to Trudell, how has white dominant society created the illusion of freedom? Why is it an illusion?
2. According to Trudell, what must white society do first in order to achieve harmony among groups in this country?
3. How does Trudell's definition of power differ from white society's concept of power?

What Do You Think?

Which part of this speech did you find especially meaningful? What made it special?

Experiencing Nonfiction

The effectiveness of Trudell's speech results from his ability to express his belief in equality for Native Americans. Choose a current issue or event that you feel strongly about. Then write a short speech in which you express your beliefs about this issue or event. Try to persuade listeners to take your position.

Optional Activity Write a brief composition or speech in which you can use a persuasive device to emphasize your main points. One persuasive device is the rhetorical question, where the speaker asks a question he or she does not expect people to answer verbally. For instance, in Trudell's speech, he asks, "does the white man oppress us, or do we oppress ourselves?"

UNIT 2: FOCUS ON WRITING

Each form of nonfiction—biography, essay, research report, news story—is unique in its purpose, audience, and tone. For instance, the purpose, audience, and tone of John Trudell's speech are very different from those of Zitkala-Ša's autobiographical sketch. However, there are certain common elements that must be considered in writing any form of nonfiction.

Writing Nonfiction

Choose one of the following nonfiction forms: biography, autobiography, news article, essay, or letter. Then write your own piece of nonfiction.

The Writing Process

Good writing requires both time and effort. An effective writer completes a number of stages that together make up the writing process. The stages of the writing process are given below to help guide you through your assignment.

Prewriting

Rather than beginning to write immediately, take some time to think about your topic. What is your topic? Can you state it in one sentence? If you cannot, perhaps it is too broad.

Consider your purpose, audience, and tone, as well as the form of nonfiction you plan to use. Is your purpose to describe, to explain, or to persuade? The purpose of Zitkala-Ša's autobiography is to describe her childhood experiences to the reader, whereas the purpose of John Trudell's speech is to persuade his audience to unite. For whom are you writing? Does your audience know a great deal about your topic or will you have to provide basic background information about it? What impression do you want to make on your audience? Should you use an informal or formal tone?

After choosing your topic, you may find that you need to gather facts and details about it. Ideas and information for writing nonfiction can come either from your own knowledge of the subject or from outside sources, such as books, magazines, films, or reference works. If you are using outside sources, take notes as you read. Remember that in preparing nonfiction, recording facts and verifying sources is crucial.

Your next step is to organize the information that you have gathered. First, write a topic sentence that identifies the specific subject you are going to write about. Then, use an outline, list, or diagram to help you plan the arrangement of the details that support your topic sentence.

Drafting and Revising

After you have organized your ideas, begin drafting your piece. A first draft need not be perfect. Rather, it is the first step in getting your ideas on paper. Use your organized outline, list, or diagram to help you arrange your topic sentence or sentences and supporting details. As you work, try not to stray too far from your original plan. However, if a good idea occurs to you while you are writing, include it in your draft. Drafting allows you the flexibility to reorganize information as you go along.

There are several points to consider when you revise nonfiction. First, make sure your topic is clear and that the details support the topic sentence. Second, eliminate details that do not relate directly to the topic. Third, make sure all your sentences are complete thoughts and that they are arranged in a logical order.

Proofreading and Publishing

After you have revised your draft, you are ready to begin proofreading. Correct any errors in spelling, grammar, punctuation, and capitalization. Then make a final copy of your work.

An important stage in the writing process is sharing what you have written with others. School newspapers, yearbooks, and class information files are just a few of the media you can use to present a piece of nonfiction to your classmates.

UNIT 3

FICTION OF THE PLAINS NATIVE AMERICANS

One main category of literature is **fiction,** which tells about imaginary characters and events. Some writers of fiction base their stories on real people and events, such as in historical fiction or science fiction, while other writers rely on their imaginations.

There are two basic forms of fiction, novels and short stories, although more specific types of fiction exist within these two broader forms. A novel is a long work of fiction. Characteristics of the novel are a complicated plot or sequence of events, a variety of major and minor characters, an important theme or message, and several different settings. A short story is a brief work of fiction. Although it often resembles a novel, the short story generally has a simpler plot and setting. It usually presents characters in one crucial moment, rather than developing them through many incidents and over a long period of time.

Fiction takes readers to another place and time. In addition, fiction explores the feelings, thoughts, and beliefs of individuals and cultures. The first selection you will read, an excerpt from N. Scott Momaday's novel *House Made of Dawn,* tells us about the Kiowa nation through the experiences of a young man who journeys to Rainy Mountain, the homeland of his grandmother. The short story "The Warriors," by Anna Lee Walters, describes the pride and painful struggles of a Pawnee family.

As you read these works of fiction, think about the methods the authors use, such as dialogue, action, and imagery, to bring these stories to life.

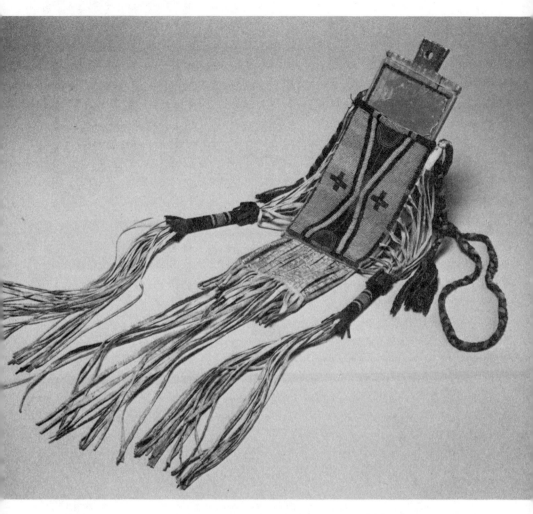

Mirror and case. *Philbrook Museum of Art,* Tulsa, Oklahoma. This mirror is encased in hide and decorated with beads and yarn. Mirrors were acquired by Crow from Europeans in trade. They were used in ceremonies to reflect light rather than images.

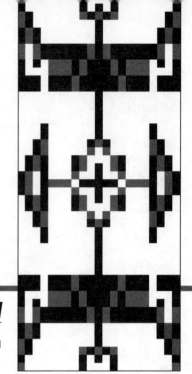

INTRODUCTION
from **House Made of Dawn**

The following excerpt is from N. Scott Momaday's novel *House Made of Dawn*. Born in Lawton, Oklahoma, Momaday is of both Kiowa and Cherokee descent. His fiction often focuses on and celebrates the traditions and beliefs of his Kiowa ancestors, who saw the land as an important part of their identity. The powerful and vivid language of his writing captures the Kiowa belief in the sacredness, beauty, and harmony of nature.

In this selection, the narrator ventures to Rainy Mountain, Oklahoma. There he visits the home and the grave of his grandmother, whom he sees as the link to his cultural history. As he wanders around the area, he connects the vast, awe-inspiring landscape of the Oklahoma plains to the stories, rituals, and traditions of the Kiowa people and to the memories of his grandmother.

from *House Made of Dawn*

by N. Scott Momaday

Tosamah,[1] orator,[2] physician, Priest of the Sun, son of Hummingbird, spoke:

"A single knoll rises out of the plain in Oklahoma, north and west of the Wichita range. For my people it is an old landmark, and they gave it the name Rainy Mountain. There, in the south of the continental trough, is the hardest weather in the world. In winter there are blizzards which come down the Williston corridor, bearing hail and sleet. Hot tornadic[3] winds arise in the spring, and in summer the prairie is an anvil's edge. The grass turns brittle and brown, and it cracks beneath your feet. There are green belts along the rivers and creeks, linear groves of hickory and pecan, willow and witch hazel. At a distance in July or August the steaming foliage seems almost to writhe in fire. Great green and yellow grasshoppers are everywhere in the tall grass, popping up like corn to sting the flesh, and tortoises crawl about on the red earth, going nowhere in the plenty of time. Loneliness is

1. **Tosamah** (TSOH-sah-mah)
2. **orator** (AWR-uht-uhr) *n.* a skilled public speaker
3. **tornadic** (tawr-NAD-ihk) *n.* like a tornado with whirling column of air

there as an aspect of the land. All things in the plain are isolate; there is no confusion of objects in the eye, but *one* hill or *one* tree or *one* man. At the slightest elevation you can see to the end of the world. To look upon that landscape in the early morning, with the sun at your back, is to lose the sense of proportion. Your imagination comes to life, and this, you think, is where Creation was begun.

"I returned to Rainy Mountain in July. My grandmother had died in the spring, and I wanted to be at her grave. She had lived to be very old and at last infirm.[4] Her only living daughter was with her when she died, and I was told that in death her face was that of a child.

"I like to think of her as a child. When she was born, the Kiowas were living the last great moment of their history. For more than a hundred years they had controlled the open range from the Smoky Hill River to the Red, from the headwaters of the Canadian to the fork of the Arkansas and Cimarron. In alliance with the Comanches, they had ruled the whole of the Southern Plains. War was their sacred business, and they were the finest horsemen the world has ever known. But warfare for the Kiowas was pre-eminently a matter of disposition[5] rather than survival, and they never understood the grim, unrelenting advance of the U.S. Cavalry. When at last, divided and ill-provisioned, they were driven onto the Staked Plain in the cold of autumn, they fell into panic. In Palo Duro Canyon they abandoned their crucial stores to pillage[6] and had nothing then but their lives. In order to save themselves, they surrendered to the soldiers at Fort Sill and were imprisoned in the old stone corral that now stands as a military museum. My grandmother was spared the humiliation of those high gray walls by eight or ten

---

4. **infirm** (ihn-FERM) *adj.* weak; feeble as from old age
5. **disposition** (dihs-puh-ZIHSH-uhn) *n.* tendency or inclination
6. **pillage** (PIHL-ihj) *v.* to loot

years, but she must have known from birth the affliction of defeat, the dark brooding of old warriors.

"Her name was Aho,[7] and she belonged to the last culture to evolve in North America. Her forebears came down from the high north country nearly three centuries ago. The earliest evidence of their existence places them close to the source of the Yellowstone River in western Montana. They were a mountain people, a mysterious tribe of hunters whose language has never been classified in any major group. In the late seventeenth century they began a long migration to the south and east. It was a journey toward the dawn, and it led to a golden age. Along the way the Kiowas were befriended by the Crows, who gave them the culture and religion of the plains. They acquired horses, and their ancient nomadic[8] spirit was suddenly free of the ground. They acquired Tai-me,[9] the sacred sun dance doll, from that moment the chief object and symbol of their worship, and so shared in the divinity of the sun. Not least, they acquired the sense of destiny, therefore courage and pride. When they entered upon the Southern Plains, they had been transformed. No longer were they slaves to the simple necessity of survival; they were a lordly and dangerous society of fighters and thieves, hunters and priests of the sun. According to their origin myth, they entered the world through a hollow log. From one point of view, their migration was the fruit of an old prophecy,[10] for indeed they emerged from a sunless world.

"I could see that. I followed their ancient way to my grandmother's grave. Though she lived out her long life in the shadow of Rainy Mountain, the immense landscape of the continental interior—all of its seasons and its sounds— lay like memory in her blood. She could tell of the Crows, whom she had never seen, and of the Black Hills, where

---

7. **Aho** (ah-HOH)
8. **nomadic** (noh-MAD-ihk) *adj.* wandering, without a fixed home
9. **Tai-me** (teye-MEE)
10. **prophecy** (PRAHF-uh-see) *n.* prediction of the future

she had never been. I wanted to see in reality what she had seen more perfectly in the mind's eye.

"I began my pilgrimage[11] on the course of the Yellowstone. There, it seemed to me, was the top of the world, a region of deep lakes and dark timber, canyons and waterfalls. But, beautiful as it is, one might have the sense of confinement there. The skyline in all directions is close at hand, the high wall of the woods and deep cleavages of shade. There is a perfect freedom in the mountains, but it belongs to the eagle and the elk, the badger and the bear. The Kiowas reckoned their stature by the distance they could see, and they were bent and blind in the wilderness.

"Descending eastward, the highland meadows are a stairway to the plain. In July the inland slope of the Rockies is luxuriant with flax and buckwheat, stonecrop and larkspur. The earth unfolds and the limit of the land recedes. Clusters of trees, and animals grazing far in the distance, cause the vision to reach away and wonder to build upon the mind. The sun follows a longer course in the day, and the sky is immense beyond all comparison. The great billowing clouds that sail upon it are shadows that move upon the grass and grain like water, dividing light. Farther down, in the land of the Crows and the Blackfeet, the plain is yellow. Sweet clover takes hold of the hills and bends upon itself to cover and seal the soil. There the Kiowas paused on their way; they had come to the place where they must change their lives. The sun is at home on the plains. Precisely there does it have the certain character of a god. When the Kiowas came to the land of the Crows, they could see the dark lees of the hills at dawn across the Bighorn River, the profusion of light on the grain shelves, the oldest deity ranging after the solstices.[12]

---

11. **pilgrimage** (PIHL-gruhm-ihj) *n.* a journey, often to a holy place
12. **solstices** (SAHL-stihs-uhs) *n.* the times of the year when the sun is farthest north or farthest south of the equator

Not yet would they veer south to the caldron of the land that lay below; they must wean their blood from the northern winter and hold the mountains a while longer in their view. They bore Tai-me in procession to the east.

"A dark mist lay over the Black Hills, and the land was like iron. At the top of a ridge I caught sight of Devils Tower—the uppermost extremity of it, like a file's end on the gray sky—and then it fell away behind the land. I was a long time then in coming upon it, and I did not see it again until I saw it whole, suddenly there across the valley, as if in the birth of time the core of the earth had broken through its crust and the motion of the world was begun. It stands in motion, like certain timeless trees that aspire too much into the sky, and imposes an illusion on the land. There are things in nature which engender[13] an awful quiet in the heart of man; Devils Tower is one of them. Man must account for it. He must never fail to explain such a thing to himself, or else he is estranged forever from the universe. Two centuries ago, because they could not do otherwise, the Kiowas made a legend at the base of the rock. My grandmother said:

Eight children were there at play, seven sisters and their brother. Suddenly the boy was struck dumb; he trembled and began to run upon his hands and feet. His fingers became claws, and his body was covered with fur. There was a bear where the boy had been. The sisters were terrified; they ran, and the bear after them. They came to the stump of a great tree, and the tree spoke to them. It bade them climb upon it, and as they did so it began to rise into the air. The bear came to kill them, but they were just beyond its reach. It reared against the tree and scored the bark all around with its claws. The seven sisters were borne into the sky, and they became the stars of the Big Dipper.

---

13. **engender** (ihn-JEN-duhr) *v.* cause

"From that moment, and so long as the legend lives, the Kiowas have kinsmen in the night sky. Whatever they were in the mountains, they could be no more. However tenuous[14] their well-being, however much they had suffered and would suffer again, they had found a way out of the wilderness.

"The first man among them to stand on the edge of the Great Plains saw farther over land than he had ever seen before. There is something about the heart of the continent that resides always in the end of vision, some essence of the sun and wind. That man knew the possible quest.[15] There was nothing to prevent his going out; he could enter upon the land and be alive, could bear at once the great hot weight of its silence. In a sense the question of survival had never been more imminent, for no land is more the measure of human strength. But neither had wonder been more accessible to the mind nor destiny to the will.

"My grandmother had a reverence for the sun, a certain holy regard which now is all but gone out of mankind. There was a wariness in her, and an ancient awe. She was a Christian in her later years, but she had come a long way about, and she never forgot her birthright. As a child, she had been to the sun dances; she had taken part in that annual rite, and by it she had learned the restoration of her people in the presence of Tai-me. She was about seven years old when the last Kiowa sun dance was held in 1887 on the Washita River above Rainy Mountain Creek. The buffalo were gone. In order to consummate the ancient sacrifice— to impale the head of a buffalo bull upon the Tai-me tree— a delegation of old men journeyed into Texas, there to beg and barter for an animal from the Goodnight herd. She was ten when the Kiowas came together for the last time as a living sun dance culture. They could find no buffalo; they had to hang an old hide from the sacred tree. That summer

---

14. tenuous (TEN-yoo-wuhs) *adj.* uncertain
15. quest (KWEST) *n.* a journey in search of something

was known to my grandmother as Ä'poto Etóda-de K'ádó,[16] Sun Dance When the Forked Poles Were Left Standing, and it is entered in the Kiowa calendars as the figure of a tree standing outside the unfinished framework of a medicine lodge.[17] Before the dance could begin, a company of armed soldiers rode out from Fort Sill under orders to disperse the tribe. Forbidden without cause the essential act of their faith, having seen the wild herds slaughtered and left to rot upon the ground, the Kiowas backed away forever from the tree. That was July 20, 1890, at the great bend of the Washita. My grandmother was there. Without bitterness, and for as long as she lived, she bore a vision of deicide.[18]

"Now that I can have her only in memory, I see my grandmother in the several postures that were peculiar to her: standing at the wood stove on a winter morning and turning meat in a great iron skillet; sitting at the south window, bent above her beadwork, and afterward, when her vision failed, looking down for a long time into the fold of her hands; going out upon a cane, very slowly as she did when the weight of age came upon her; praying. I remember her most often at prayer. She made long, rambling prayers out of suffering and hope, having seen many things. I was never sure that I had the right to hear, so exclusive were they of all mere custom and company. The last time I saw her, she prayed standing by the side of her bed at night, . . . the light of a kerosene lamp moving upon her dark skin. Her long black hair, always drawn and braided in the day, lay upon her shoulders . . . like a shawl. I did not always understand her prayers; I believe they were made of an older language than that of ordinary speech. There was something inherently sad in the sound, some slight hesitation upon the syllables of sorrow. She began in

---

16. **Ä'poto Etóda-de K'ádó** name of the Sun Dance
17. **medicine lodge** *n.* a building where religious rites are performed
18. **deicide** (DEE-uh-seyed) *n.* the killing of a god

a high and descending pitch, exhausting her breath to silence; then again and again—and always the same intensity of effort, of something that is, and is not, like urgency in the human voice. Transported so in the dim and dancing light among the shadows of her room, she seemed beyond the reach of time, as if age could not lay hold of her. But that was illusion; I think I knew then that I should not see her again.

"Houses are like sentinels in the plain, old keepers of the weather watch. There, in a very little while, wood takes on the appearance of great age. All colors soon wear away in the wind and rain, and then the wood is burned gray and the grain appears and the nails turn red with rust. The windowpanes are black and opaque; you imagine there is nothing within, and indeed there are many ghosts, bones given up to the land. They stand here and there against the sky, and you approach them for a longer time than you expect. They belong in the distance; it is their domain.

"My grandmother lived in a house near the place where Rainy Mountain Creek runs into the Washita River. Once there was a lot of sound in the house, a lot of coming and going, feasting and talk. The summers there were full of excitement and reunion. The Kiowas are a summer people; they abide the cold and keep to themselves, but when the season turns and the land becomes warm and vital they cannot hold still; an old love of going returns upon them. The old people have a fine sense of pageantry[19] and a wonderful notion of decorum.[20] The aged visitors who came to my grandmother's house when I was a child were men of immense character, full of wisdom and disdain. They dealt in a kind of infallible quiet and

---

19. pageantry (PAJ-uhn-tree) *n.* gorgeous display
20. decorum (dih-KAWR-uhm) *n.* good taste in behavior and speech

gave but one face away; it was enough. They were made of lean and leather, and they bore themselves upright. They wore great black hats and bright ample shirts that shook in the wind. They rubbed fat upon their hair and wound their braids with strips of colored cloth. Some of them painted their faces and carried the scars of old and cherished enmities. They were an old council of war lords, come to remind and be reminded of who they were. Their wives and daughters served them well. The women might indulge themselves; gossip was at once the mark and compensation of their servitude.[21] They made loud and elaborate talk among themselves, full of jest and gesture, fright and false alarm. They went abroad in fringed and flowered shawls, bright beadwork and German silver.[22] They were at home in the kitchen, and they prepared meals that were banquets.

"There were frequent prayer meetings, and great nocturnal feasts. When I was a child, I played with my cousins outside, where the lamplight fell upon the ground and the singing of the old people rose up around us and carried away into the darkness. There were a lot of good things to eat, a lot of laughter and surprise. And afterward, when the quiet returned, I lay down with my grandmother and could hear the frogs away by the river and feel the motion of the air.

"Now there is a funeral silence in the rooms, the endless wake of some final word. The walls have closed in upon my grandmother's house. When I returned to it in mourning, I saw for the first time in my life how small it was. It was late at night, and there was a white moon, nearly full. I sat for a long time on the stone steps by the

---

21. **servitude** (SER-vuh-tood) *n.* being under someone's control
22. **German silver** a silver colored mixture of copper, zinc, and nickel

kitchen door. From there I could see out across the land; I could see the long row of trees by the creek, the low light upon the rolling plains, and the stars of the Big Dipper. Once I looked at the moon and caught sight of a strange thing. A cricket had perched upon the handrail, only a few inches away from me. My line of vision was such that the creature filled the moon like a fossil. It had gone there, I thought, to live and die, for there of all places was its small definition made whole and eternal. A warm wind rose up and purled[23] like the longing within me.

"The next morning I awoke at dawn and went out of my grandmother's house to the scaffold of the well that stands near the arbor.[24] There was a stillness all around, and night lay still upon the pecan groves away by the river. The sun rose out of the ground, powerless for a long time to burn the air away, dim and nearly cold like the moon. The orange arc grew upon the land, curving out and downward to an impossible diameter. It must not go on, I thought, and I began to be afraid; then the air dissolved and the sun backed away. But for a moment I had seen to the center of the world's being. Every day in the plains proceeds from that strange eclipse.

"I went out on the dirt road to Rainy Mountain. It was already hot, and the grasshoppers began to fill the air. Still, it was early in the morning, and birds sang out of the shadows. The long yellow grass on the mountain shone in the bright light, and a scissortail[25] hied above the land. There, where it ought to be, at the end of a long and legendary way, was my grandmother's grave. She had at last succeeded to that holy ground. Here and there on the dark stones were the dear ancestral names. Looking back once, I saw the mountain and came away."

---

23. **purled** (PERLD) *v.* moved in ripples with a murmuring sound
24. **arbor** (AR-buhr) *n.* a place shaded by trees or shrubs
25. **scissortail** (SIHZ-er-tayl) *n.* a bird with a forked tail

AFTER YOU READ

Exchanging Backgrounds and Cultures

1. What does this selection reveal about the history and traditions of the Kiowa culture?
2. In which Kiowa customs does Momaday remember his grandmother participating?
3. How do you think the Kiowas' deep respect for the land differs from the mainstream culture's relationship to nature?

What Do You Think?

Which image or memory in this selection was especially meaningful to you? Why was it special?

Experiencing Fiction

According to the Kiowas' beliefs of origin, they entered the world through a dark, hollow log, which explains their reverence for the sun's light. Write a brief story about the origins of your ancestors and how they relate to the beliefs of your culture. Base the story on your knowledge of your cultural history or on a creative idea of your own.

Optional Activity Write a brief story in which the setting—the time and place of the action—plays an important part in the plot. For example, in Momaday's story, he uses the dramatic setting of Rainy Mountain to express the Kiowas' connection to the land.

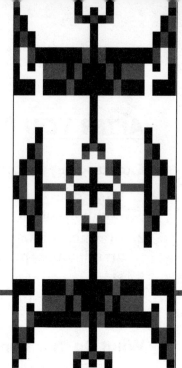

INTRODUCTION
The Warriors

As a member of the Pawnee nation and as a writer and teacher on a Navajo reservation, Anna Lee Walters speaks first to a Native American audience about the historical and cultural connections among all Native American nations. Her many lectures, books, and articles have also educated people of other cultures about the beliefs and traditions of Native Americans.

Historically, the Pawnees took great pride in their skills as warriors, dominating the plains in what is now Nebraska. Their religious beliefs center on the power and beauty of natural elements, such as the wind and storms, which they perceive to be messengers of the great Father, Tirawa. The following short story, "The Warriors," explores the experiences of two Native American sisters who learn about their Pawnee heritage through their uncle's traditional songs, stories, and prayers, as well as through his fighting spirit.

The Warriors

by Anna Lee Walters

In our youth, we saw hobos[1] come and go, sliding by
our faded white house like wary cats who did not want us
too close. Sister and I waved at the strange procession of
passing men and women hobos. Just between ourselves,
Sister and I talked of that hobo parade. We guessed at and
imagined the places and towns we thought the hobos
might have come from or had been. Mostly they were
White or Black people. But there were Indian hobos, too.
It never occurred to Sister and me that this would be
Uncle Ralph's end.

Sister and I were little, and Uncle Ralph came to visit
us. He lifted us over his head and shook us around him
like gourd rattles. He was Momma's younger brother, and
he could have disciplined us if he so desired. That was part
of our custom. But he never did. Instead, he taught us
Pawnee words. "*Pari*[2] is Pawnee and *pita*[3] is man," he said.
Between the words, he tapped out drumbeats with his

---

1. **hobos** (HOH-bohz) *n.* homeless people who travel from place to
   place
2. *Pari* (PAH-ree)
3. *pita* (PEE-tuh)

fingers on the table top, ghost dance and round dance songs that he suddenly remembered and sang. His melodic voice lilted over us and hung around the corners of the house for days. His stories of life and death were fierce and gentle. Warriors dangled in delicate balance.

He told us his version of the story of *Pahukatawa*,[4] a Skidi[5] Pawnee warrior. He was killed by the Sioux, but the animals, feeling compassion for him, brought *Pahukatawa* to life again. "The Evening Star and the Morning Star bore children and some people say that these offspring are who we are," he often said. At times he pointed to those stars and greeted them by their Pawnee names. He liked to pray for Sister and me, for everyone and every tiny thing in the world, but we never heard him ask for anything for himself from *Atius*,[6] the Father.

"For beauty is why we live," Uncle Ralph said when he talked of precious things only the Pawnees know. "We die for it, too." He called himself an ancient Pawnee warrior when he was quite young. He told us that warriors must brave all storms and odds and stand their ground. He knew intimate details of every battle the Pawnees ever fought since Pawnee time began, and Sister and I knew even then that Uncle Ralph had a great battlefield of his own.

As a child I thought that Uncle Ralph had been born into the wrong time. The Pawnees had been ravaged so often by then. The tribe of several thousand when it was at its peak over a century before were then a few hundred people who had been closely confined for more than a

---

4. **Pahukatawa** (pah-hoo-kah-TAH-wah) *n.* name of a Pawnee warrior
5. **Skidi** (SKIH-dee) *n.* name of a group of Pawnee
6. **Atius** (AH-tee-uhs) *n.* a spiritual being

hundred years. The warrior life was gone. Uncle Ralph was trapped in a transparent bubble of a new time. The bubble bound him tight as it blew around us.

Uncle Ralph talked obsessively[7] of warriors, painted proud warriors who shrieked poignant battle cries at the top of their lungs and died with honor. Sister and I were little then, lost from him in the world of children who saw everything with children's eyes. And though we saw with wide eyes the painted warriors that he fantasized and heard their fierce and haunting battle cries, we did not hear his. Now that we are old and Uncle Ralph has been gone for a long time, Sister and I know that when he died, he was tired and alone. But he was a warrior.

The hobos were always around in our youth. Sister and I were curious about them, and this curiosity claimed much of our time. They crept by the house at all hours of the day and night, dressed in rags and odd clothing. They wandered to us from the railroad tracks where they had leaped from slow-moving boxcars[8] onto the flatland. They hid in high clumps of weeds and brush that ran along the fence near the tracks. The hobos usually traveled alone, but Sister and I saw them come together, like poor families, to share a can of beans or a tin of sardines that they ate with sticks or twigs. Uncle Ralph also watched them from a distance.

One early morning, Sister and I crossed the tracks on our way to school and collided with a tall, haggard whiteman. He wore a very old-fashioned pin-striped black jacket covered with lint and soot. There was fright in his eyes when they met ours. He scurried around us, quickening his pace. The pole over his shoulder where his

---

7. **obsessively** (uhb-SES-ihv-lee) *adj.* without being able to stop
8. **boxcars** *n.* enclosed freight cars that are part of a train

possessions hung in a bundle at the end bounced as he nearly ran from us.

"Looks just like a scared jackrabbit," Sister said, watching him dart away.

That evening we told Momma about the scared man. She warned us about the dangers of hobos as our father threw us a stern look. Uncle Ralph was visiting but he didn't say anything. He stayed the night and Sister asked him, "Hey, Uncle Ralph, why do you suppose they's hobos?"

Uncle Ralph was a large man. He took Sister and put her on one knee. "You see, Sister," he said, "hobos are a different kind. They see things in a different way. Them hobos are kind of like us. We're not like other people in some ways and yet we are. It has to do with what you see and feel when you look at this old world."

His answer satisfied Sister for a while. He taught us some more Pawnee words that night.

Not long after Uncle Ralph's explanation, Sister and I surprised a Black man with white whiskers and fuzzy hair. He was climbing through the barbed-wire fence that marked our property line. He wore faded blue overalls with pockets stuffed full of handkerchiefs. He wiped sweat from his face. When it dried, he looked up and saw us. I remembered what Uncle Ralph had said and wondered what the Black man saw when he looked at us standing there.

"We might scare him," Sister said softly to me, remembering the whiteman who had scampered away.

Sister whispered, "Hi," to the Black man. Her voice was barely audible.

"Boy, it's sure hot," he said. His voice was big and he smiled.

"Where are you going?" Sister asked.

"Me? Nowheres, I guess," he muttered.

"Then what you doing here?" Sister went on. She was

bold for a seven-year-old kid. I was older but I was also quieter. "This here place is ours," she said.

He looked around and saw our house with its flowering mimosa trees and rich green mowed lawn stretching out before him. Other houses sat around ours.

"I reckon I'm lost," he said.

Sister pointed to the weeds and brush further up the road. "That's where you want to go. That's where they all go, the hobos."

I tried to quiet Sister but she didn't hush. "The hobos stay up there," she said. "You a hobo?"

He ignored her question and asked his own. "Say, what is you all? You not Black, you not White. What is you all?"

Sister looked at me. She put one hand on her chest and the other hand on me. "We Indians!" Sister said.

He stared at us and smiled again. "Is that a fact?" he said. "Know what kind of Indians we are?" Sister asked him.

He shook his fuzzy head. "Indians is Indians, I guess," he said.

Sister wrinkled her forehead and retorted.[9] "Not us! We not like others. We see things different. We're Pawnees. We're warriors!"

I pushed my elbow into Sister's side. She quieted.

The man was looking down the road and he shuffled his feet. "I'd best go," he said.

Sister pointed to the brush and weeds one more time. "That way," she said.

He climbed back through the fence and brush as Sister yelled, "Bye now!" He waved a damp handkerchief. Sister and I didn't tell Momma and Dad about the Black man. But much later Sister told Uncle Ralph every word that had been exchanged with the Black man. Uncle Ralph listened and smiled.

---

9. **retorted** (rih-TAWRT-uhd) *v.* answered

Months later when the warm weather had cooled and Uncle Ralph came to stay with us for a couple of weeks, Sister and I went to the hobo place. We had planned it for a long time. That afternoon when we pushed away the weeds, not a hobo was in sight.

The ground was packed down tight in the clearing among the high weeds. We walked around the encircling brush and found folded cardboards stacked together. Burned cans in assorted sizes were stashed under the cardboards, and there were remains of old fires. Rags were tied to the brush, snapping in the hard wind.

Sister said, "Maybe they're all in the boxcars now. It's starting to get cold."

She was right. The November wind had a bite to it and the cold stung our hands and froze our breaths as we spoke.

"You want to go over to them boxcars?" she asked. We looked at the Railroad Crossing sign where the boxcars stood.

I was prepared to answer when a voice roared from somewhere behind us.

"Now, you young ones, you git on home! Go on! Git!"

A man crawled out of the weeds and looked angrily at us. His eyes were red and his face was unshaven. He wore a red plaid shirt with striped gray and black pants too large for him. His face was swollen and bruised. An old woolen pink scarf hid some of the bruise marks around his neck, and his topcoat was splattered with mud.

Sister looked at him. She stood close to me and told him defiantly, "You can't tell us what to do! You don't know us!"

He didn't answer Sister but tried to stand. He couldn't. Sister ran to him and took his arm and pulled on it. "You need help?" she questioned.

He frowned at her but let us help him. He was tall. He seemed to be embarrassed by our help.

"You Indian, ain't you?" I dared to ask him.

He didn't answer me but looked at his feet as if they could talk so he wouldn't have to. His feet were in big brown overshoes.

"Who's your people?" Sister asked. He looked to be about Uncle Ralph's age when he finally lifted his face and met mine. He didn't respond for a minute. Then he sighed. "I ain't got no people," he told us as he tenderly stroked his swollen jaw.

"Sure you got people. Our folks says a man's always got people," I said softly. The wind blew our clothes and covered the words.

But he heard. He exploded like a firecracker. "Well, I don't! I ain't got no people! I ain't got nobody!"

"What you doing out here anyway?" Sister asked. "You hurt? You want to come over to our house?"

"Naw," he said. "Now you little ones, go on home. Don't be walking round out here. Didn't nobody tell you little girls ain't supposed to be going round by themselves? You might git hurt."

"We just wanted to talk to hobos," Sister said.

"Naw, you don't. Just go on home. Your folks is probably looking for you and worrying bout you."

I took Sister's arm and told her we were going home. Then we said "Bye" to the man. But Sister couldn't resist a few last words, "You Indian, ain't you?"

He nodded his head like it was a painful thing to do. "Yeah, I'm Indian."

"You ought to go on home yourself," Sister said. "Your folks probably looking for you and worrying bout you."

His voice rose again as Sister and I walked away from him. "I told you kids, I don't have no people!" There was exasperation[10] in his voice.

---

10. exasperation (ihg-ZAS-puh-ray-shuhn) *n.* great annoyance

Sister would not be outdone. She turned and yelled. "Oh yeah? You Indian ain't you? Ain't you?" she screamed. "We your people!"

His topcoat and pink scarf flapped in the wind as we turned away from him.

We went home to Momma and Dad and Uncle Ralph then. Uncle Ralph met us at the front door. "Where you all been?" he asked looking toward the railroad tracks. Momma and Dad were talking in the kitchen.

"Just playing, Uncle," Sister and I said simultaneously.[11]

Uncle Ralph grabbed both Sister and I by our hands and yanked us out the door. "*Awkuh!*" he said, using the Pawnee expression to show his dissatisfaction.

Outside, we sat on the cement porch. Uncle Ralph was quiet for a long time, and neither Sister nor I knew what to expect.

"I want to tell you all a story," he finally said. "Once, there were these two rats who ran around everywhere and got into everything all the time. Everything they were told not to do, well they went right out and did. They'd get into one mess and then another. It seems that they never could learn."

At that point Uncle Ralph cleared his throat. He looked at me and said, "Sister, do you understand this story? Is it too hard for you? You're older."

I nodded my head up and down and said, "I understand."

Then Uncle Ralph looked at Sister. He said to her, "Sister, do I need to go on with this story?"

Sister shook her head from side to side. "Naw, Uncle Ralph," she said.

"So you both know how this story ends?" he said gruffly. Sister and I bobbed our heads up and down again.

---

11. **simultaneously** (seye-muhl-TAY-nee-uhs-lee) *adv.* at the same time

We followed at his heels the rest of the day. When he tightened the loose hide on top of his drum, we watched him and held it in place as he laced the wet hide down. He got his drumsticks down from the top shelf of the closet and began to pound the drum slowly.

"Where you going, Uncle Ralph?" I asked. Sister and I knew that when he took his drum out, he was always gone shortly after.

"I have to be a drummer at some doings tomorrow," he said.

"You a good singer, Uncle Ralph," Sister said. "You know all them old songs."

"The young people nowadays, it seems they don't care bout nothing that's old. They just want to go to the Moon." He was drumming low as he spoke.

"We care, Uncle Ralph," Sister said.

"Why?" Uncle Ralph asked in a hard, challenging tone that he seldom used on us.

Sister thought for a moment and then said, "I guess because you care so much, Uncle Ralph."

His eyes softened as he said, "I'll sing you an *Eruska*[12] song, a song for the warriors."

The song he sang was a war dance song. At first Sister and I listened attentively, but then Sister began to dance the man's dance. She had never danced before and tried to imitate what she had seen. Her chubby body whirled and jumped the way she'd seen the men dance. Her head tilted from side to side the way the men moved theirs. I laughed aloud at her clumsy effort, and Uncle Ralph laughed heartily, too.

Uncle Ralph went in and out of our lives after that. We heard that he sang at one place and then another, and people come to Momma to find him. They said

---

12. *Eruska* (uh-RUS-kah)

that he was only one of a few who knew the old ways and the songs.

When he came to visit us, he always brought something to eat. The Pawnee custom was that the man, the warrior, should bring food, preferably meat. Then, whatever food was brought to the host was prepared and served to the man, the warrior, along with the host's family. Many times Momma and I, or Sister and I, came home to an empty house to find a sack of food on the table. Momma or I cooked it for the next meal, and Uncle Ralph showed up to eat.

As Sister and I grew older, our fascination with the hobos decreased. Other things took our time, and Uncle Ralph did not appear as frequently as he did before.

Once while I was home alone, I picked up Momma's old photo album. Inside was a gray photo of Uncle Ralph in an army uniform. Behind him were tents on a flat terrain. Other photos showed other poses but only in one picture did he smile. All the photos were written over in black ink in Momma's handwriting. *Ralphie in Korea,* the writing said.

Other photos in the album showed our Pawnee relatives. Dad was from another tribe. Momma's momma was in the album, a tiny gray-haired woman who no longer lived. And Momma's momma's dad was in the album; he wore old Pawnee leggings and the long feathers of a dark bird sat upon his head. I closed the album when Momma, Dad, and Sister came home.

Momma went into the kitchen to cook. She called me and Sister to help. As she put on a bibbed apron, she said, "We just came from town, and we saw someone from home there." She meant someone from her tribal community.

"This man told me that Ralphie's been drinking hard," she said sadly. "He used to do that quite a bit a long time ago, but we thought it had stopped. He seemed to be all right for a few years." We cooked and then ate in silence.

Washing the dishes, I asked Momma, "How come Uncle Ralph never did marry?"

Momma looked up at me but was not surprised by my question. She answered, "I don't know, Sister. It would have been better if he had. There was one woman who I thought he really loved. I think he still does. I think it had something to do with Mom. She wanted him to wait."

"Wait for what?" I asked.

"I don't know," Momma said, and sank into a chair. . . .

He finally came to the house once when only I happened to be home. He was haggard and tired. His appearance was much like that of the whiteman that Sister and I met on the railroad tracks years before.

I opened the door when he tapped on it. Uncle Ralph looked years older than his age. He brought food in his arms. "*Nowa*, Sister," he said in greeting. "Where's the other one?" He meant my sister.

"She's gone now, Uncle Ralph. School in Kansas," I answered. "Where you been, Uncle Ralph? We been worrying about you."

He ignored my question and said, "I bring food. The warrior brings home food. To his family, to his people." His face was lined and had not been cleaned for days. He smelled of cheap wine.

I asked again, "Where you been, Uncle Ralph?"

He forced himself to smile. "Pumpkin Flower," he said, using the Pawnee name, "I've been out with my warriors all this time."

He put one arm around me as we went to the kitchen table with the food. "That's what your Pawnee name is. Now don't forget it."

"Did somebody bring you here, Uncle Ralph, or are you on foot?" I asked him.

"I'm on foot," he answered. "Where's your Momma?"

I told him that she and Dad would be back soon. I started to prepare the food he brought.

Then I heard Uncle Ralph say, "Life is sure hard sometimes. Sometimes it seems I just can't go on."

"What's wrong, Uncle Ralph?" I asked.

Uncle Ralph let out a bitter little laugh. "What's wrong?" he repeated. "What's wrong? All my life, I've tried to live what I've been taught, but Pumpkin Flower, some things are all wrong!"

He took a folded pack of Camel cigarettes from his coat pocket. His hand shook as he pulled one from the pack and lit the end. "Too much drink," he said sadly. "That stuff is bad for us."

"What are you trying to do, Uncle Ralph?" I asked him.

"Live," he said.

He puffed on the shaking cigarette a while and said, "The old people said to live beautifully with prayers and song. Some died for beauty, too."

"How do we do that, Uncle Ralph, live for beauty?" I asked.

"It's simple, Pumpkin Flower," he said. "Believe!"

"Believe what?" I asked.

He looked at me hard. "*Awkuh!*" he said. "That's one of the things that is wrong. Everyone questions. Everyone doubts. No one believes in the old ways anymore. They want to believe when it's convenient, when it doesn't cost them anything and they get something in return. There are no more believers. There are no more warriors. They are all gone. Those who are left only want to go to the Moon." . . .

In the years that followed, Uncle Ralph saw us only when he was sober. He visited less and less. When he did show up, he did a tapping ritual on our front door. We welcomed the rare visits. Occasionally he stayed at our house for a few days at a time when he was not drinking. He slept on the floor.

He did odd jobs for minimum pay but never complained about the work or money. He'd acquired a vacant look in his eyes. It was the same look that Sister and I had seen in the hobos when we were children. He wore a similar careless array of clothing and carried no property with him at all.

The last time he came to the house, he called me by my English name and asked if I remembered anything of all that he'd taught me. His hair had turned pure white. He looked older than anyone I knew. I marvelled at his appearance and said, "I remember everything." That night I pointed out his stars for him and told him how *Pahukatawa* lived and died and lived again through another's dreams. I'd grown, and Uncle Ralph could not hold me on his knee anymore. His arm circled my waist while we sat on the grass.

He was moved by my recitation[13] and clutched my hand tightly. He said, "It's more than this. It's more than just repeating words. You know that, don't you?"

I nodded my head. "Yes, I know. The recitation is the easiest part but it's more than this, Uncle Ralph."

He was quiet, but after a few minutes his hand touched my shoulder. He said, "I couldn't make it work. I tried to fit the pieces."

"I know," I said.

"Now before I go," he said, "do you know who you are?"

The question took me by surprise. I thought very hard. I cleared my throat and told him, "I know that I am fourteen. I know that it's too young."

"Do you know that you are a Pawnee?" he asked in a choked whisper.

---

13. recitation (res-uh-TAY-shuhn) *n.* a speech

"Yes Uncle," I said.

"Good," he said with a long sigh that was swallowed by the night.

Then he stood and said, "Well, Sister, I have to go. Have to move on."

"Where are you going?" I asked. "Where all the warriors go?" I teased.

He managed a smile and a soft laugh. "Yeah, wherever the warriors are, I'll find them."

I said to him, "Before you go, I want to ask you . . . Uncle Ralph, can women be warriors too?"

He laughed again and hugged me merrily. "Don't tell me you want to be one of the warriors too?"

"No, Uncle," I said, "Just one of yours." I hated to let him go because I knew I would not see him again.

He pulled away. His last words were, "Don't forget what I've told you all these years. It's the only chance not to become what everyone else is. Do you understand?"

I nodded and he left.

I never saw him again.

The years passed quickly. I moved away from Momma and Dad and married. Sister left before I did.

Years later in another town, hundreds of miles away, I awoke in a terrible gloom, a sense that something was gone from the world the Pawnees knew. The despair filled days, though the reason for the sense of loss went unexplained. Finally, the telephone rang. Momma was on the line. She said, "Sister came home for a few days not too long ago. While she was here and alone, someone tapped on the door, like Ralphie always does. Sister yelled, 'Is that you, Uncle Ralphie? Come on in.' But no one entered."

Then I understood that Uncle Ralph was dead. Momma probably knew too. She wept softly into the phone.

Later Momma received an official call confirming

Uncle Ralph's death. He had died from exposure[14] in a hobo shanty,[15] near the railroad tracks outside a tiny Oklahoma town. He'd been dead for several days and nobody knew but Momma, Sister, and me.

Momma reported to me that the funeral was well attended by the Pawnee people. Uncle Ralph and I had said our farewells years earlier. Momma told me that someone there had spoken well of Uncle Ralph before they put him in the ground. It was said that "Ralphie came from a fine family, an old line of warriors."

Ten years later, Sister and I visited briefly at Momma's and Dad's home. We had been separated by hundreds of miles for all that time. As we sat under Momma's flowering mimosa trees, I made a confession to Sister. I said, "Sometimes I wish that Uncle Ralph were here. I'm a grown woman but I still miss him after all these years."

Sister nodded her head in agreement. I continued. "He knew so many things. He knew why the sun pours its liquid all over us and why it must do just that. He knew why babes and insects crawl. He knew that we must live beautifully or not live at all."

Sister's eyes were thoughtful, but she waited to speak while I went on. "To live beautifully from day to day is a battle all the way. The things that he knew are so beautiful. And to feel and know that kind of beauty is the reason that we should live at all. Uncle Ralph said so. But now, there is no one who knows what that beauty is or any of the other things that he knew."

Sister pushed back smoky gray wisps of her dark hair. "You do," she pronounced. "And I do, too."

---

14. **exposure** (ihk-SPOH-zhuhr) *n.* without having shelter
15. **shanty** (SHAN-tee) *n.* a shack

"Why do you suppose he left us like that?" I asked.

"It couldn't be helped," Sister said. "There was a battle on."

"I wanted to be one of his warriors," I said with an embarrassed half-smile.

She leaned over and patted my hand. "You are," she said. Then she stood and placed one hand on her bosom and one hand on my arm. "We'll carry on," she said.

I touched her hand resting on my arm. I said, "Sister, tell me again. What is the battle for?"

She looked down toward the fence where a hobo was coming through. We waved at him.

"Beauty," she said to me. "Our battle is for beauty. It's what Uncle Ralph fought for, too. He often said that everyone else just wanted to go to the Moon. But remember, Sister, you and I done been there. Don't forget, after all, we're children of the stars."

AFTER YOU READ

Exchanging Backgrounds and Cultures

1. What kinds of battles do you think Uncle Ralph fights as a Pawnee warrior?

2. In what ways do the sisters carry on their uncle's battles?

3. What does Uncle Ralph reveal about his attitude toward the hobos? How are the Pawnees and the hobos alike? How are they different?

What Do You Think?

Which character or scene in this short story interested you most? Why was it especially meaningful for you?

Experiencing Fiction

"The Warriors" centers on the two sisters' relationship with their Uncle Ralph. Write a short story about a relative of whom you are especially fond. Focus the story on the ways this relationship influences your beliefs and behaviors. Remember to include some dialogue in the story.

Optional Activity Think about someone who is especially interesting to you and jot down the qualities that make this person notable. Create a fictional character who has some of the same personality traits you listed. Then write a brief story, focusing on showing this character's personality through his or her thoughts, dialogue, and actions.

UNIT 3: FOCUS ON WRITING

Fiction, which includes novels and short stories, tells about imaginary characters and events. However, writers of fiction bring their personal experiences to the creative process. They often base a particular character or situation on one with which they are familiar. For instance, N. Scott Momaday's novel, *House Made of Dawn,* takes place in Oklahoma, where he was born and raised, and focuses on the traditions and beliefs of his Kiowa ancestors.

Writing a Short Story

Write a short story in which one or more characters are caught up in a conflict.

The Writing Process

Good writing requires both time and effort. An effective writer completes a number of stages that together make up the writing process. The stages of the writing process are given below to help guide you through your assignment.

Prewriting

You can come up with an idea for a short story in several ways. You can base it on a personal experience, on a historical event, or on an imaginary situation. While planning your story, make a chart with a column for each of the five major elements in a story: setting, characters, conflict, plot, and theme. Then focus on one element and build your story around it. As you come up with specific ideas for each element, place them in the appropriate column.

Although your story may not include every point or idea below, the following questions can help you to develop the various parts of your story before you begin to write.

Setting: Where does the story take place? During what year and season does the action occur? What images will you use to reveal the setting?

Characters: Who will be the main character, or protagonist? What other characters will take part in the action? How will you reveal the personality of each character?

Conflict: What is the central conflict? Is it internal (within the character's mind) or external (between the character and some outside force)? In "The Warriors," the conflict is both internal and external, as the narrator struggles to preserve her family's traditional beliefs and values in a modern society.

Plot: What events will take place? In what order will they occur? What event will spark the central conflict? What will be the high point, or climax, of the story? How will the conflict be resolved?

Theme: Will the story have a message for the reader? How will the story reveal this message or theme?

Another decision to make before you begin to write is who the narrator of the story will be. For instance, the narrator can be a character in the story, as in "The Warriors."

Drafting and Revising

Use your prewriting chart to write a draft of your story. Remember that the first draft need not be perfect. Include dialogue and vivid imagery as well as special techniques, such as flashback and suspense.

When revising a short story, use only essential descriptions and dialogue. Eliminate any unnecessary details that might confuse the reader. It is also time to come up with a title that will attract the readers' interest and reveal an important detail about the story.

Proofreading and Publishing

Next, proofread your revision for any errors in spelling, grammar, capitalization, and puncutation. Then make a neat final copy of your work.

You are now ready to share your story. Read it aloud to your classmates, family, and friends. Submit your story to your school's literary magazine. If your school does not have a magazine, try starting one with your classmates.

UNIT 4

POETRY OF THE PLAINS NATIVE AMERICANS

Poetry is perhaps the most condensed form of literature. Because poems are generally shorter than novels, short stories, or dramas, poets must create meaning with fewer words. Most poets use a variety of literary devices, such as imagery, repetition, and figurative language, to convey meaning.

Imagery refers to a poet's use of words to create mental pictures, or images, that capture experience. An image may appeal to any one of the five senses, although in literature, visual images are the most common. **Repetition** is the repeated use of any sound, word, or grammatical structure. In poetry, repetition helps to create rhythm. Two important types of repetition are **alliteration** (uh-lit-uh-RAY-shuhn) and **parallelism. Figurative language** is language that uses figures of speech. A figure of speech is a way of saying one thing to mean another. Two important figures of speech are **simile** and **metaphor**.

Poems are usually divided into lines and stanzas. In the past, poems were usually written in regular rhythmical patterns, or **meters**. However, many poets have begun to use **free verse**, which is not written in any special form and doesn't require rhyme or rhythm.

You will notice that the poets in this unit use a number of these methods to bring their poems to life. In the first group of poems, the writers mainly use imagery and metaphor as they reflect on their cultural identity. The poets in the second group use a wide variety of devices to express their connection to the past. As you read, see if you can identify the specific literary devices in each poem.

Prairie Fire. *Philbrook Museum of Art,* Tulsa, Oklahoma. Well-known watercolor done in the Santa Fe Studio style. Hunters and antelope fleeing from approaching fire. Painted by Kiowa Comanche artist Blackbear Bosin.

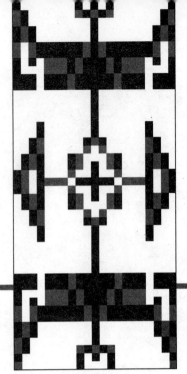

INTRODUCTION

Section 1: Reflections

The group of poems you are about to read presents four poets who describe the struggle of Native Americans to preserve their culture.

In "The Man from Washington," James Welch captures the sense of separation his people feel from mainstream society. Born in Browning, Montana, in 1940, Welch is of Blackfeet and Gros Ventre descent. Best known as a novelist, Welch's work often examines the emptiness of reservation life. Similarly, Lance Henson's poem "Extinction" focuses on the destruction of Native American culture. Henson, a Cheyenne from Calumet, Oklahoma, writes frequently about Native American themes.

In Louise Erdrich's poem "Indian Boarding School: The Runaways," the speaker describes the shame and loneliness she suffers in a Native American boarding school. Born in Little Falls, North Dakota, Erdrich is a member of the Turtle Mountain Chippewa nation and is widely known for her fiction.

Joy Harjo, author of "Morning Once More," explores the power and beauty of the morning sun, a symbol of rebirth and continuation. Born in the heart of the Creek Nation in Tulsa, Oklahoma, Harjo often captures in her poetry the spirituality of the Creek culture.

The Man from Washington

by James Welch

The end came easy for most of us.
Packed away in our crude beginnings
in some far corner of a flat world,
we didn't expect much more
than firewood and buffalo robes
to keep us warm. The man came down,
a slouching dwarf with rainwater eyes,
and spoke to us. He promised
that life would go on as usual,
that treaties would be signed, and everyone—
man, woman and child—would be inoculated
against a world in which we had no part,
a world of money, promise and disease.

Indian Boarding School:[1] The Runaways

by Louise Erdrich

Home's the place we head for in our sleep.
Boxcars[2] stumbling north in dreams
don't wait for us. We catch them on the run.
The rails, old lacerations[3] that we love,
shoot parallel across the face and break
just under Turtle Mountains. Riding scars
you can't get lost. Home is the place they cross.

The lame guard strikes a match and makes the dark
less tolerant. We watch through cracks in boards
as the land starts rolling, rolling till it hurts
to be here, cold in regulation clothes.
We know the sheriff's waiting at midrun
to take us back. His car is dumb and warm.
The highway doesn't rock, it only hums
like a wing of long insults. The worn-down welts
of ancient punishments lead back and forth.

1. **boarding school** Many Native American children were sent away
   to schools run by the government or private organizations.
2. **Boxcars** enclosed freight cars that are part of a train
3. **lacerations** (las-uh-RAY-shuhnz) *n.* wounds, injuries

All runaways wear dresses, long green ones,
the color you would think shame was. We scrub
the sidewalks down because it's shameful work.
Our brushes cut the stone in watered arcs
and in the soak frail outlines shiver clear
a moment, things us kids pressed on the dark
face before it hardened, pale, remembering
delicate old injuries, the spines of names and leaves.

Extinction

by Lance Henson

along the bleak
            sun
                brow
day goes out alone

we lift our eyes to
the same
nothingness

in my hands i hold

the last
      aching
            sparrow

who
remembers
me

Morning Once More

by Joy Harjo

the sun over the horizon
a sweating yellow horse
our continuance
        the uncountable distance
that sweeps through our hands
the first prayers
        in the morning
it is this that i believe in
the galloping sun
and my whole life
        a rider

AFTER YOU READ

Exchanging Backgrounds and Cultures

1. Which lines in Welch's poem "The Man from Washington" and in Henson's poem "Extinction" best express the loss of Native American culture? Briefly explain your answer.

2. Which images in the poems of Harjo and Henson reflect their connection to nature? What do these images suggest about the poets' values?

3. In what ways do Erdrich's and Welch's poems show how mainstream society has forced itself on Native American culture?

What Do You Think?

Which poem or poems in this group did you find especially meaningful? How did the poetic form, rhythm, and imagery influence your decision?

Experiencing Poetry

Using free verse, write a short poem that has a theme that concerns life in modern society. First, prepare a list of images that you associate with modern life. Then, use this list to develop your poem. Structure your verse to re-create the rising and falling rhythms of natural speech. Vary the lengths of the lines for emphasis.

Optional Activity Remember that a metaphor is a figure of speech in which one thing is spoken of as though it were something else. For instance, in Joy Harjo's poem, she uses the metaphor of a horse to represent the sun's warmth, energy, and movement. Write a short poem that contains a metaphor to draw a connection between two elements in nature.

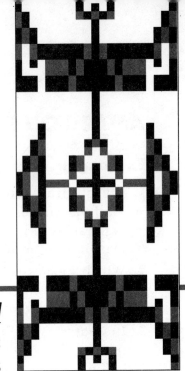

INTRODUCTION

Section 2:
Living in Two Worlds

The poets in this section, Living in Two Worlds, look to their ancestors and the traditional beliefs of their culture as a way to better understand themselves and their place in the world. You will notice that the first three poems are written by women and therefore share certain images and themes. Like weavers whose designs reflect their natural surroundings, these poets weave together the threads of their cultural history to create the fabric of their present lives.

The first poem by Joy Harjo, "Remember," explores the connection between the cycles of nature and the cycles of human life. Similarly, Annette Arkeketa West's poem "Calumet Early Evening" examines the connectedness of life. Much like Harjo, West hears the voices of her Otoe and Creek ancestors in the whistling wind. Finally, Paula Gunn Allen, who is of Laguna Pueblo, Lakota, and Lebanese descent, uses the image of weaving in her poem "Grandmother" to represent the creation and continuation of life.

In the last poem, "Driving in Oklahoma," Carter Revard explores the sharp contrast between the values of contemporary society and the values of his Osage heritage.

Remember

by Joy Harjo

Remember the sky that you were born under,
know each of the star's stories.
Remember the moon, know who she is. I met her
in a bar once in Iowa City.
Remember the sun's birth at dawn, that is the
strongest point of time. Remember sundown
and the giving away to night.
Remember your birth, how your mother struggled
to give you form and breath. You are evidence of
her life, and her mother's, and hers.
Remember your father. He is your life, also.
Remember the earth whose skin you are:
red earth, black earth, yellow earth, white earth
brown earth, we are earth.
Remember the plants, trees, animal life who all have their
tribes, their families, their histories, too. Talk to them,
listen to them. They are alive poems.
Remember the wind. Remember her voice. She knows the
origin of this universe. I heard her singing Kiowa war

dance songs at the corner of Fourth and Central once.
Remember that you are all people and that all people
are you.
Remember that you are this universe and that this
universe is you.
Remember that all is in motion, is growing, is you.
Remember that language comes from this.
Remember the dance that language is, that life is.
Remember.

Calumet[1] *Early Evening*

by Annette Arkeketa West

Your name grows across
fields of cotton and alfalfa
against boards
which saturate voices
of ghost wind
settling over river trees

The chant of an old woman
in evening shadow
unwrapping thin black braids
calling you home
calling you home

---

1. **Calumet** (KAL-yuh-met) *n.* a town in Oklahoma

Grandmother

by Paula Gunn Allen

Out of her own body she pushed
silver thread, light, air
and carried it carefully on the dark, flying
where nothing moved.

Out of her body she extruded
shining wire, life, and wove the light
on the void.

From beyond time,
beyond oak trees and bright clear water flow,
she was given the work of weaving the strands
of her body, her pain, her vision
into creation, and the gift of having created,
to disappear.

After her,
the women and the men weave blankets into tales of life,
memories of light and ladders,
infinity-eyes, and rain.
After her I sit on my laddered rain-bearing rug
and mend the tear with string.

Driving in Oklahoma

by Carter Revard

On humming rubber along this white concrete
  lighthearted between the gravities
of source and destination like a man
      halfway to the moon
    in this bubble of tuneless whistling
at seventy miles an hour from the windvents,
        over prairie swells rising
    and falling, over the quick offramp
that drops to its underpass and the truck
      thundering beneath as I cross
with the country music twanging out my windows,
      I'm grooving down this highway feeling
technology is freedom's other name when
      —a meadowlark
    comes sailing across my windshield
      with breast shining yellow
   and five notes pierce
     the windroar like a flash
    of nectar on mind
gone as the country music swells up and
    drops me wheeling down
   my notch of cement-bottomed sky
   between home and away
      and wanting
to move again through country that a bird
  has defined wholly with song
      and maybe next time see how
he flies so easy, when he sings.

AFTER YOU READ

Exchanging Backgrounds and Cultures

1. What do the women in Harjo's poem "Remember" and in Allen's poem "Grandmother" represent? What common image do both of these poets use to capture the significance of women?
2. What role do Native American songs play in the poems of Harjo and West?
3. How do the poems of West and Revard reveal the relationship between human life and nature?

What Do You Think?

Which poem or poems in this section were especially meaningful to you? What thoughts and feelings did they awaken in you?

Experiencing Poetry

In "Driving in Oklahoma," the speaker observes the Oklahoma landscape as he travels in his car. Write a poem about a journey that you have made. List some of the things you observed during your journey. Using these concrete images, write a short poem that conveys the meaning of the experience.

Optional Activity Write a poem about a personal experience, an important event, or an element of nature. Use parallelism to establish a pattern. In poetry, parallelism often links related ideas and establishes a pattern. For instance, in Harjo's poem, she begins most sentences with the word *remember*, which connects all living things to each other and creates the poem's rhythm.

UNIT 4: FOCUS ON WRITING

Poems use figurative language and imagery to express feelings and concepts such as truth and beauty. Like other forms of literature, poems can tell stories, too.

Writing a Poem

Consider the following topics: a sport, a season, a person, a scene, an animal, a special place. Then, write a poem about one of these topics or another topic of your choice.

The Writing Process

Good writing requires both time and effort. An effective writer completes a number of stages that together make up the writing process. The stages of the writing process are given below to help guide you through your assignment.

Prewriting

Brainstorm to explore the subject you have chosen. Use clustering or cubing to generate details about your topic. In a cluster diagram, details branch outward from a central idea allowing you to see the relationships among ideas. Cubing (so-named because a cube has six sides) allows you to examine your subject from different points of view. To discover the six sides of a subject, describe it, compare it, associate it, analyze it, apply it, and argue for or against it.

After you have generated images that correspond to your subject, think about the message, or theme, of your poem. The theme should relate to the details included in the poem.

Next, think about tone. In poetry, the tone is usually revealed through the setting, the imagery, and the word choice. For instance, in Lance Henson's poem "Extinction," the sad, gloomy tone is reflected in words and images like "the bleak sun," "nothingness," and "the last aching sparrow."

Finally, consider the form of the poem. How many stanzas will it have? How will the words be arranged on the page? The form can greatly influence the rhythm, tone, and meaning of your poem. In Joy Harjo's "Morning Once More," the shortness and position of the last line force the reader's attention to the image of "a rider."

Drafting and Revising

Now that you have chosen the topic, images, theme, tone, and form of your poem, it is time to get the first draft down on paper. When drafting a poem, let your ideas flow naturally. Using figurative language, such as metaphors and similes, can enhance the overall effect of the poem. Certain sound devices, like alliteration, the repetition of consonant sounds at the beginnings of words or accented syllables, help to create a poem's pattern or rhythm. For instance, in the first stanza of "Calumet Early Evening," the repetition of the "s" sound gives the poem a hypnotic rhythm and dreamlike mood. With these techniques in mind, draft your poem several more times.

Now, select the best version of your poem and begin to revise it. First, examine the poem's immediate impact. How does it make you feel? Next, consider the details of the poem. Have the words you used created the desired effect?

Choose a title for the poem. The title can reflect the subject of the poem, or it can add to the poem's mystery!

Proofreading and Publishing

Now, proofread your poem for any errors in spelling, grammar, punctuation, and capitalization. In poetry, it is acceptable to purposely use noncustomary punctuation and capitalization.

Poems are especially fun to read aloud. Hold a poetry reading in your class. You could also submit your poem to the school literary magazine or to a national student magazine. Perhaps you would like to create a classroom collection that includes the poems of your classmates.

UNIT 5

DRAMA OF THE PLAINS NATIVE AMERICANS

Drama has much in common with other types of literature. Like fiction and poetry, drama expresses themes and makes use of special devices, such as imagery and figurative language. Like novels and short stories, dramas also have plots, conflicts, settings, and characters.

In one important way, drama differs from all other types of literature. Dramas are written to be performed by actors in front of an audience. You will notice that the printed form reflects this fact, as each page contains dialogue and stage directions. The dialogue is made up of the lines the actors speak. The stage directions describe how the actors should speak and move; how the stage should look; what movable pieces, or "props," should be used by the actors; and what kind of lighting and sound effects should be used during the performance.

Dramas are usually divided into smaller sections, much like a novel is divided into chapters. An act is a major section in a drama. Within an act, there are smaller sections called scenes. The drama you are about to read, *49*, can be viewed as one long act containing a number of scenes.

The writer of *49*, Hanay Geiogamah, combines traditional dramatic methods with new forms. The inclusion of songs from a variety of Native American nations, as well as elements of Native American speech within the English dialogue, enhances the drama's theme of Native American unity. While you read the following drama, try to imagine what it would be like to hear the characters speak their lines and to see the action on a stage.

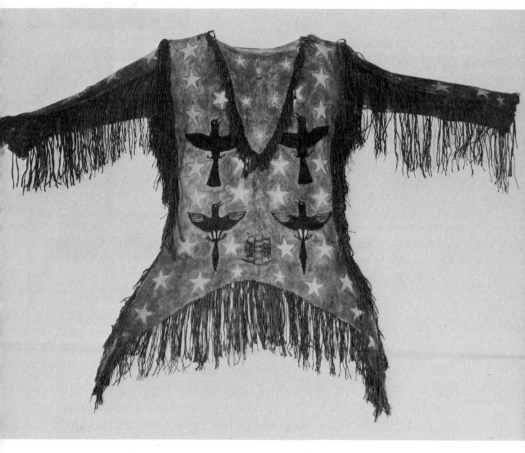

Arapaho Ghost Dance Shirt. *National Museum of the American Indian, Smithsonian Institution.* The shirt is made of buckskin and decorated with birds and stars. It was believed to protect the wearer from harm.

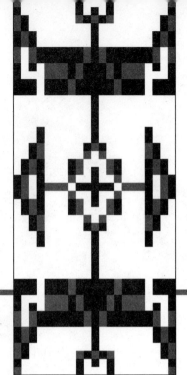

INTRODUCTION

49

Hanay Geiogamah, a Native American playwright and director, was born in Lawton, Oklahoma. Although he is a Kiowa, he writes plays for and about Native Americans from a variety of cultures. He incorporates Kiowa words and the music of Navajo, Taos, Apache, and other nations into his plays.

The following play, *49*, strongly conveys this message of Native American unity. A 49 is a celebration in which young Native Americans come together to enjoy the traditions of their heritage and to renew their sense of identity. The play is a series of scenes that alternately present the ritual of the 49 and the distrustful attitude of the police witnessing the event. In the play, Geiogamah links the past, present, and future of Native American culture through the figure of the Night Walker, who can move supernaturally through time. Although the Night Walker warns the young people of a potentially threatening future, an idea reinforced by the presence of the police, he remains optimistic and hopeful.

49

by Hanay Geiogamah

The People of the Play

NIGHT WALKER, ceremonial leader of the tribe, can be any
    age
BALLADEER, a young Indian singer of today
MEMBERS OF THE 49 GROUP
HIGHWAY PATROLMAN
SPIRITS
YOUNG PEOPLE OF THE TRIBE
YOUNG DUDE BY THE CAR
SINGING MAN; BOY AND GIRL OF THE TRIBE
WEAVING WOMAN; GIRLS OF THE TRIBE
YOUTHS IN CAR: GIRL DRIVER; PASSENGERS; GIRL IN BACK SEAT
OLD LADY VISITOR FROM FAR AWAY
CHIEFS
YOUNG WARRIORS
PEOPLE OF THE TRIBE
LEAD SINGERS AND DRUMMERS OF THE 49
TWO FIGHTING DUDES AND THEIR GIRLFRIENDS
49 LEAD MAN

Setting: A ceremonial ground circa 1885 and the same ceremonial ground in the present.

Music and Songs of the Play

SCENE 1:   UTE FLUTE CALLING SONG
SCENE 2:   DANCING AND SINGING 49;
          THEY DON'T KNOW WHY THOSE DAMNED
          PATROLS WON'T LEAVE 'EM ALONE
SCENE 3:   SIOUX MEDICINE CHANT
SCENE 4:   WATER-WHISTLES SONG (instrumental)
SCENE 5:   YA-KA-MA-DA 49;
          JUST WHEN WE GET TOGETHER, SWEETHEART
SCENE 6:   POLLEN ROAD
SCENE 8:   KIOWA TURTLE SONG
SCENE 9:   OH YES, I LOVE YOU, HONEY
SCENE 11: A YAH HEY A YAH FIGHT IT OUT!
          COMING AND GOING
SCENE 12: POLLEN ROAD (reprise)

An experienced traditional drummer (or drummers), willing to experiment with varied rhythms, must attend all rehearsals to assist in developing the music for the production and to devise a pattern of drum rhythms that can extend throughout the entire performance at varied tempos and levels to provide a taut structure for the play. The music can employ bells, rattles, ratchets, bull-roarers, Apache violins, flutes, whistles, various sizes of drums, piano, and guitars.

Author's Note

A 49 celebration usually begins about midnight or just after, when the more formal activities of the powwow or Indian fair or tribal celebration are over. There is a loosely structured pattern of time and movement in the formation of a 49 congregation. Forty-nines always take place at night; really good ones go on until sunrise and after. More young people are involved than older ones, and thus the scene is charged with the energy of hundreds of youths. . . .

Scene 1

A single light reveals a dance area of tightly packed earth with trees, grass, and bushes growing alongside. There are brush arbors in the background, and a roadway extends out of the area. A high embankment[1] rises above the roadway, and more trees are in back of this. Other lights start to come up with the Ute Flute Calling Melody, which floats through the night air. The lights progressively illumine[2] other corners of this ceremonial area, a much-used site with a long history of many tribespeople coming and going. Night Walker enters slowly, moves around the area with poise and dignity, gesturing expansively.

NIGHT WALKER

Greetings. Hello. Good day to you.
Greetings. Hello. Good day to you.

I, Night Walker, spiritual leader of the tribe, our people, speak to all of the young people of the tribe, our people.

Will you hear my voice?

---

1. **embankment** (em-BANK-muhnt) *n.* a large pile of earth used to keep back water or to hold up a roadway
2. **illumine** (ih-LOO-muhn) *v.* to light up

Will you hear my voice?

Hear me, Night Walker. I have a thing of very strong purpose to say to you. It is a thing of deepest concern for the tribe, our people.

I ask all of the young men and women of the tribe, our people, to come to the ceremonial circle, to our people's arbor, so that I may speak with you.

I will pray for all of you there. I will tell you of this purpose.

(now with more urgency)

The tribe, our people, need you!
The tribe, our people, need you!

(moving off now)

Thank you.
Thank you.

The flute melody fades as the lights dim out.

Scene 2

A *sudden, jagged crackle of a two-way police radio breaks the calm. The lights on the set are shifting gently, magically.*

PATROL VOICE 1
Unit 9? Unit 9? This is Unit 4. Do you read me?

PATROL VOICE 2

> I read you, Unit 4.

PATROL VOICE 1

> I'm sittin' solid three miles west, two miles north of
> the Apache Y.

PATROL VOICE 2

> Ain't seen none yet. City says they're a-drivin' around
> town like ants. Hunnerds of 'em. More'n all week. Lot
> of 'em from out of town. It always gets kind-ee wild
> t'ord the end of this fair, but this year seems wilder
> than ever.

PATROL VOICE 1

> Yep, it's perty wild. Got sixty-five of 'em in the county
> jail and all filled up in the city. Every . . . one of 'em's
> under age. Can't pay their fines. We'll get us a bunch
> more of 'em tonight, I betcha.

PATROL VOICE 2

> I have an idee they'll be a-headin' for the old
> Whitehorse Road tonight. They claim that lil' dance
> ground out there's Indian property and that no law
> officers can trespass or arrest a Indian there.

PATROL VOICE 1

> Trespass my . . . *(He laughs.)*

PATROL VOICE 2

> *(with surprise)* Hey! Boy! One just went by . . . loaded
> down! Left front out. I'm a-following.

*A spotlight locates the Balladeer. A single car headlight hits the
roadway directly in a flash as lights reveal youths packed into a
car, a mixed lot, obviously en route to a 49.*

BALLADEER

    COME ON, DANCE 49, HONEY
    COME ON, DANCE WITH ME
    COME ON, DANCE 49, HONEY
    COME ON, DANCE WITH ME.

    TEACH YOU HOW TO SING TURTLE SONG, HONEY

    SHOW YOU HOW TO DANCE WITH ME
    TEACH YOU HOW TO SING TURTLE SONG, HONEY
    SHOW YOU HOW TO DANCE WITH ME.

    I GOT A DRUM
    LET'S MAKE A SONG
    I'LL SING TO YOU, HONEY
    ALL NIGHT LONG.

    TAKE YOU DOWN TO ANADARKO WITH ME, HONEY
    TAKE YOU OUT TO TAHLEQUAH
    UP TO THE OSAGE COUNTRY FOR THE POWWOWS
    HONEY COME ON BLAZE WITH ME
    HONEY COME ON BLAZE WITH ME.

    COME ON DANCE 49, HONEY
    COME ON SING WITH ME
    COME ON DANCE 49, HONEY
    COME ON, BE WITH ME.
    (*light out on Balladeer.*)

YOUTH IN CAR
    (*looking back*) . . . cops!

The 49 group mimes the car as they careen around the environment, the lights following their movements. The Balladeer moves about, following their progress, and begins to sing accompaniment as the police give chase with red lights flashing.

BALLADEER

THEY DON'T KNOW WHY THOSE . . . PATROLS
WON'T LEAVE 'EM ALONE
HO WAY YAW HEY YEY
THEY DON'T KNOW WHY THOSE . . . PATROLS
WON'T LEAVE 'EM ALONE
HOWAY YAW HEY
HO WAY YAW HEY YEY EY YO!

THEY WANT TO TAKE 'EM ALL TO JAIL
HO WAY YAW HEY
HO WAY YAW HEY YEY
LOCK 'EM UP
GIVE 'EM HELL
HO WAY YAW HEY
HO WAY YAW HEY YEY EY YO.

DIS/OR/DER/LY AND DRUNK/EN/NESS
HO WAY YAW HEY
HO WAY YAW HEY YEY
THIRTY DAYS!
HO WAY YAW HEY
HO WAY
HO WAY
HO WAY YAW HEY YEY EY YO!

BUT THEY CAN ALL GO STRAIGHT TO HELL!
HO WAY YAW HEY
HO WAY YAW HEY YEY
STRAIGHT TO HELL!
HO WAY YAW HEY
HO WAY
HO WAY
HO WAY YAW HEY YEY EY YO!

The 49 group dive for cover in the underbrush to escape the police and take positions of hiding. A police car search-light scans the terrain slowly, fades out.

Scene 3

Lights reveal Night Walker, whose body is making the motions of a journey through rugged terrain. Odd flashes of light illuminate his progress, which is being observed by masks and faces of humans and animals. The 49 group are in their hiding positions throughout the scene. Night Walker reaches a clearing, composes himself, and delivers a prayer that is directed as much to himself as to the power spirits.

NIGHT WALKER

I heed as unto those I call.
I heed as unto those I call.
Send to me thy potent aid.

Help us, the tribe, our people, oh, holy place around.
Help us, our friends, our brothers and sisters. We heed as unto thee we call.

I come to visit with my brothers and sisters.
Will you hear my voice?

Will you hear my voice? The voice of a friend who has honor and respect deep in his heart for you?

I am the oldest man of the tribe, our people. You, my brothers and sisters, have given me this honor of life.

The masks and faces and supernatural activities become larger.

You know my voice. We sing together. You were at my birth. You know my father. You know my father's father, and you know his father. You are kind and generous to all of us, the tribe, our people.

Will I sing for you now? I will tell you a story of a bear who comes to watch the dancing of the tribe, our people. (*pause*) Some of the people say the bear is learning our songs.

I have brought food for my friends. I will make a meal for us. I will make a fire. I will spread my blankets.

He does these things.

I have tobacco with me. It is good tobacco.

I have sage[3] that was brought to the tribe our people from a place far away from our home. I will burn it for you.

He waits, then lights the sage.

I saw a young man and a young girl of the tribe our people the other day. (*pause*) They both were smiling and happy. I looked at them for a long time. I watched them walk about. I saw in their smiles the signs of a family of wonderful hunters and weavers.

I had a feeling to speak with them, but I . . . did . . . not.

The faces move closer.

The faces of these two young ones appear before me now. I bring their smiles here for my friends to see.

I am made sad . . . by . . . these smiles. My friends!

I am the youngest man of the tribe, our people. You, my brothers and sisters have given me this honor.

Haw!
Haw!
I know.
I hope.
I pray.

---

3. sage (SAYJ) *n.* a plant in the mint family used as an herb or as an ornamental plant

He has established communication.

> I dream.
> I smile.
> I do.
> Haw!
> I know the smiles.
> I see.
> I am the oldest man of the tribe. Haw! Haw!
> The young ones' smiles are my smiles.
> It is I who am smiling.
> I am the girl.
> I am the boy.
> Yes.
> They will both know that I am they.

A longer pause. A jew's harp and Apache violin[4] are heard.

> The men chiefs of the tribe, our people, do not look to me when they talk with me of the things that concern the good of the tribe, our people.
>
> They do not tell me all that they want me to know.
>
> When they return to the tribe, our people, after fighting with the enemies, I must talk more and more to Brother Death.
>
> I must ask Brother Death . . . to . . . take the spirits . . . of the young men . . . who have stopped living . . . with us.
>
> Haw! I wait.
> Haw!
> I see.
> I see. Brother Death sees too. How long? How far?

---

4. **Apache violin** a one-stringed instrument that makes a sound like a single note repeated on a violin

He lights more sage, then the young people begin, with soft voices, the Sioux Medicine Chant, and sing it as a counter-point to Night Walker's prayer.

I have come here for the young man whose smiles I see.
I have come here for the young woman, who is so
pretty.
I have come here for the warrior chiefs who will not
look at me.
I am the oldest man of the tribe.
I have come here as two smiles who cannot see into
the darkness that I see, gathering ahead on our road.

Must Brother Death direct their eyes? (*very firmly*)

Must all life be taken from us?
My friends know.

I do not know about the smiling faces of the young
man and the young woman of the tribe, our people.

I do not know how long the young people will know
the smell of the sage and the cedar.

I sing. Will they sing? Many beautiful songs?
I dance. How will they know to dance?
I make pictures of color. Will they see this beauty?

I conduct the ceremonies of our journey. Which one
of them will follow me to lead?

I heal my sister's child. Will they know the medicine of
the tribe, our people?

I have learned the way of Brother Winter and I talk
with our brothers in the grass and trees and in the sky.
Will they know these friends?

I am the oldest man of the tribe, our people, and I
give help to my brothers and sisters in our journey.

The answer is completed.

> They will hear my voice. They will hear your voices.
> They will look to me. They will look to you.

> We live a very long time. They will live a very long
> time. I am not afraid. I will not stop walking. I will not
> stop singing. I will not stop dancing. I will talk to all of
> my friends for a very long time. We will walk through
> the dark that *has* passed us, the tribe, our people. A-ho!
> A-ho, pah-bes. A-ho.

> We will live and walk together for a long time. All of us
> will live and walk together for a long time.

He bows deeply and remains in the position as the Sioux Medicine Chant builds, then fades to end the scene. His exit is like a disappearance.

Scene 4

*I*n the darkness a youth strikes a match and draws it slowly toward his face, illuminating his features until he whistles softly, blowing it out.

Other matches and whistles begin to dot the scene.

The 49 group one by one come out of their hiding positions and begin circling in an effort to find each other.

The Water-whistles Song is heard as this night ballet unfolds.

They find their friends and partners, stand together in small groups, check the night air for a feeling of safety.

When the group has re-formed, the song, which has no words, ends. All lights go to a blue shading to complete the scene.

Scene 5

T*he dance arena is dimly lit, quiet. Car lights appear moving on in the distance. Sounds of car motors are heard mixed with sounds of the night. Other lights rise slowly, gently; deep patches of color flow through the setting to contrast with the night sky. The images of a caravan of Indian cars come into focus. Dust, noise, a sense of gathering. Flutes, bells are heard as members of the 49 group filter into the area of the dance ground. The colors of the lights now begin to look dazzling. The elation of the participants grows as they claim the area as their own for the 49. Night Walker sits above the action, observing calmly. Two youths enter with a dance drum and pause in the circle center. A third youth lights a match to heat the head of the drum for tuning. The 49 Balladeer appears atop the embankment and a drum roll echoes as he begins to sing.*

BALLADEER

    YAH HEY YAAH
    YAH HEY YAAH
    HEY EY YAH EY YA HO
    EY YAH HEY
    YAH EY YAH HEY YEY
    YAH EY YAH HO
    EY YAH HEY
    YAH EY YAH HO
    EY YAH HEY
    EY YAH HEY
    EY YO
    YA KA MA DA 49!

He repeats the vocables, then the 49 group join in Ya-ka-ma-da 49 and dance with powerful drive. When the singing ends, the drumming rolls to a stop with whooping and yelling, begins again immediately with another drum roll, and the Balladeer leads off another song.

BALLADEER

> JUST WHEN WE GET TOGETHER, SWEETHEART
> WE'LL SING AND DANCE ALL NIGHT
> AND THEN WE'LL ROCK TO THE 49
> HEY O YAH HO EY YAH HEY EY YAH HEY YO!

The 49, with its restless movements, its shifting images and special sounds, comes fully to life.

PATROL VOICE 1

> *(as 49 activities surge)* This is Unit 4. Unit 4 to Units 5, 6, 7, and 8. Come in, Units 5, 6, 7, and 8. Do you read me? (*They check in.*) Unit 9 reports fifty or more cars in the area of the old Whitehorse Road, nine mile west, two mile north. Repeat, 49's starting on the old Whitehorse Road, nine mile west, two mile north. Red '64 Chevy four-door sedan parked on the westbound side about a mile up from the turn-off, abandoned there by twelve to fourteen Indian youths. Nine says more cars're comin' in from the west by a off-county road line. Units 5, 6, 7, 8, advise to proceed to the area. Call check thirty minutes. Repeat, call check thirty minutes. Over.

The drumbeat continues as the lights fade slowly on youths moving in and out of the round dance.

Scene 6

*T*he young people of the tribe are assembled to hear Night Walker. Parents and relatives may be watching at a distance. Note: The young tribal members are costumed for an earlier *era, and they conduct themselves in the manner of students of Night Walker.*

NIGHT WALKER
> (*in full command*)
> I tell you of things I know.
> I tell you of things I see.
> I tell you to prepare you
> For all that is coming.
> For a loss
> That will be like death to our people.

Consternation among the young people; he lets them settle down.

> Soon, we will live in a different land.
> I cannot see this place.
>
> Soon, we will be forced from our arbor.
>
> Soon, the singing will stop.
> Soon, there will be no dancing.
> The pipe will not burn.
> We will forget our stories.
> We will not meet our friends.

Harsh red lights reveal a field littered with buffalo skeletons and bones. These images intermingle with the shadows of the young people.

> Soon, we will not have the things that make our way
> the way we know.
> Soon, all our hearts will feel this pain.
>
> Soon, the tribe, our people, will be told that we
> cannot do anything they do not want us to do.
>
> Soon, we will sit in the grass and wonder where we are
> going.
>
> Soon, we will close our eyes to not see what will be
> before them.

You will ask yourselves who you are.

If I knew why this must be I would tell you.

You will know.

The death images fade.

YOUNG PEOPLE
   (in unison[5]) We will follow you, grandfather, you show
   us the way.

The Pollen Road melody is heard in the distance.

NIGHT WALKER
   Sing with me. I will lead you.
   Dance along with me. I will show you the steps.
   Know how we came to this place.
   Know the stories of our way.
   Know the way I know, and I will follow you.
   We will follow you.
   You will lead.
   Do not be afraid to make new songs.

YOUNG PEOPLE
   We will walk by you
   Through times of suffering and sorrow
   To a life for us that will be new.

NIGHT WALKER
   You must lead our clan
   To a time of understanding
   When a man will not hurt a man
   By killing his way of living.

---

5. in unison (IHN YOO-nuh-suhn) together, at the same time

YOUNG PEOPLE
>   We move out onto the plain.
>   We begin this journey.
>   We will endure the pain.
>   We take the pipe, the tipi.

NIGHT WALKER
>   I pray for you.
>   I sing for you.
>   I smoke for you.
>   I give to you
>   These things.
>   You give them life.

He distributes a drum, a fan, feathers. The Pollen Road melody and chant intensify. The drumbeat builds to a sharp pitch, then rolls down.

YOUNG PEOPLE
>   HEY AH NAH HEY NAY
>   HEY AH NAH HEY NAY
>   HEY AH NAH HEY NAY
>   HEY AH NAH HEY NAY OH
>
>   WALKING TO THE EAST
>   EVERYTHING IS BEAUTIFUL
>   WALKING TO THE WEST
>   EVERYTHING IS BEAUTIFUL
>   WALKING TO THE NORTH
>   EVERYTHING IS BEAUTIFUL
>   WALKING TO THE SOUTH
>   EVERYTHING IS BEAUTIFUL
>
>   HEY AH NAH HEY NAY
>   HEY AH NAH HEY NAY
>   HEY AH NAH HEY NAY
>   HEY AH NAH HEY NAY OH
>
>   WALKING DOWN THAT POLLEN ROAD
>   EVERYTHING IS BEAUTIFUL

WALKING DOWN THAT POLLEN ROAD
EVERYTHING IS BEAUTIFUL

HEY AH NAH HEY NAY
HEY AH NAH HEY NAY
HEY AH NAH HEY NAY OH

They move about the environment, then form a circle and raise their faces upward.

PATROL VOICE 1

Unit 4? Unit 4? Come in, Unit 4. This is Unit 6. Unit 6. Do you read me? Over.

PATROL VOICE 2

This is Unit 4. I read you, Unit 6.

PATROL VOICE 1

I'm sittin' solid a mile back east of the Whitehorse turnoff. There's no activity this side of 62. Nothing north either. Over.

PATROL VOICE 2

Sit solid, Unit 6. I'd say there's more'n 300 cars down in there now. Five, 7, 8, and 9'll have to go in with us. Over.

PATROL VOICE 1

Roger. Sittin' solid. You give the call. Over.

Lights fade on the circle of young people.

Scene 7

Several youths surround the front of one of the cars. The 49 movements form a low-key background. A seventeen- or eighteen-year-old holds the center of attention in the group. He speaks solo.

YOUTH

> *(to one of group)* Hey, guy, how many you think's here?
> 'Bout two thousand! Geeyall, heey!
> I wonder how many of 'em's snaggin'! Geeyall!
> I'll, uh, I'll break 'em all up with a good one, aaah!
> Which one can ya'll sing? A good one, heeey!
> I wanna' lead a really good one, geeyall.
> Which one? I need practice before I hit, geeyall. I can
> lead good, guy.
> Which one?
> Birdlegs?
> Birdlegs? Geeyall, a old one.

He pretends to drum on the car hood. Others in the group are in a playful mood too.

YOUTH

> Who's gonna' second me? Which one of you,
> geeyall?
> Birdlegs, a old one. Birdlegs Special. Geeyall!

He play-drums again on the car hood, realizing he is losing the group's attention.

YOUTH

> *(suddenly, with wide grin and delight)* KAY TASS AH YOK
> AH ME DAH QUASSS! AAAHHHH! GEEEYALLL!

Laughter from the group.

YOUTH

> *(still happy)* Yeah, it's a old one. I know it. Geeeyalll!

Lights transfer to dancers, then dim out.

Scene 8

Night Walker is speaking to a group of the young tribespeople underneath the arbor. The Singing Man is instructing a second group around a large drum, and some young girls listen to Weaving Woman, who sits beside a weaving loom. Sounds of camp life and its activities are heard in the background.

SINGING MAN

Our people have had these gifts since before our long journey here. The mother gave the tribe, our people, this drum. For us its sound is the sound of her heart beating with life.

He describes the flute, the bells, and the rattles. This is done in mime;[6] none of his words are heard by the audience. He then gives the drumsticks to a boy and a girl, and they slowly begin to beat a rhythm.

BOY

(shyly, lightening the beat) A song came to me the other day when I was by the river. It is a short song, about a turtle.

SINGING MAN

Turtles are my good friends. They have fun at night when their other friends are sleeping. Sing your song.

---

6. **mime** (MEYEM) *n.* acting out an action without using words

BOY

> (*halting*) AH NAH HEY MAH ... (*He stops, looks at the girl, nudges her to join.*) She knows it too. I taught her.

SINGING MAN

> Good. Sing the turtle song. I'll sing it with you, if you teach me.

BOY AND GIRL

> AH NAH HEY MAH/KONE KEEN GYA HON SAY/MYONG YAH HEY/PEENG PONE GYA/EY YAH HEY EY YAH HEY EY YO.

SINGING MAN

> If the turtle can give you such a song, you can find many more beautiful ones almost everywhere you look, yes?

GIRL

> We have a song that we sing to each other.

SINGING MAN

> My woman has found many songs for me. I sing for her by the campfire at night.
> (*He beats the drum softly, outlining a song.*) Will you sing for me the song you have for each other?

BOY

> It is a good song, but it is not finished yet.

SINGING MAN

> I know many songs which are not finished. They are still songs. Sing.

BOY

> I will finish the song now. Will you help me? I want to take this song with me to the new place where we will live.

The Singing Man looks to Night Walker, who looks down at the scene.

SINGING MAN
Yes. Sing.

BOY
If you will drum.

SINGING MAN
You drum. You will feel your song more if you do.

The boy adds vocables to his words, The Kiowa Turtle Song, sings it through, then repeats it in full. The Singing Man joins him.

ENTIRE GROUP
AH NAH HEY MAH
KONE KEEN
GYA HON SAY
MYONG YAH HEY
PEENG PONE GYA
EY YAH HEY
EY YAH HEY EY YO.

SINGING MAN
Our music is everywhere. You can find it wherever you look. It can find you too. When a song comes to you, learn it. Learn it and give it to others. And do not forget to thank the turtle for his song, or your hearts for their music. Always show that you are thankful for the gift of music. It is a wonderful blessing. The people will always have songs if . . . you . . . sing.

Lights transfer to the weaving circle.

WEAVING WOMAN
(*as she displays a beautiful blanket*) I have had this design since my mother gave it to me many years ago. She took the pattern from the red ants as they make their

way. She wove some of her own hair into the design so that a part of her could be with the blanket as long as the blanket lives.

FIRST GIRL
Will . . . I keep . . . my design . . . for my children and for their children?

WEAVING WOMAN
It will be yours, and theirs, and ours, if you make it so beautiful that nobody else can duplicate its beauty. The tribe will be honored for the beauty you create.

SECOND GIRL
(*hesitantly*) But . . . our way . . . is . . . is . . . changing. How will we make our designs live in the blankets if we have no . . . sheep to give us wool for the loom?

WEAVING WOMAN
(*after a pause*) A design can live and grow for many years before it is placed on the loom. You can always see it . . . when you close your eyes. You can change the colors, line them up in other patterns. You can have many different designs. They will be happy to wait if you promise them that you will keep them until there is . . . wool . . . for the . . . looms.

A single spot illuminates the blanket; all other lights down soft.

PATROL VOICE 1
Seven and eight, do you read me?

PATROL VOICE 2
Seven reads.

PATROL VOICE 3
Eight reads.

PATROL VOICE 1
Sittin' solid.

PATROL VOICE 2
> Sittin' solid.

PATROL VOICE 3
> Sittin' solid.

The spot fades slowly on the blanket, then out.

Scene 9

*T*he lights isolate a group of eight youths packed tightly into a small car, searching for the 49. . . . The girl driving the car is very eager to reach the scene. A drumbeat paces the scene and builds steadily to the climax.

DRIVER
> . . . I thought they all went to T-Bird Hill.

YOUTH
> The law's probably got there first.

DRIVER
> . . . we're 'bout outa gas.

GIRL IN BACK SEAT
> Well, hell, slow down! You're goin' too fast.
> We'll get there.

DRIVER
> We got enough to get to Moonlight.

GIRL IN BACK SEAT
> Well, slow down.

The driver switches on the car radio, flips stations, and lights a cigarette as others in the car shift, giggle, embrace.

DRIVER
> How far is Moonlight from T-Bird?

YOUTH

Forty-nine thousand miles! Aaiiee. (*laughter from all*)

GIRL

. . . slow down. You don't even know where you're goin'!

DRIVER

I'm not goin' too fast. I wanna' get there. I gotta' find you-know-who before he finds you-know-who.

GIRL

Aw, he'll be there. Be careful.

DRIVER

(*approaching a turn in the road*) Which way do I turn? Left?

YOUTH

Yeah, left, then straight for 'bout six miles.

DRIVER

(*adjusting after turning*) Oh, . . . it's almost two. He's probably already snagged that . . . ugly thing.

She accelerates;[7] others shift places, become tense.

YOUTH

(*to driver*) It's only 'bout four more miles. You gotta turn right after that sign on that mile corner road. You better slow down a little bit, cops might be parked down that way.

GIRL

Yeah, slow down!

DRIVER

I'm all right, I'm drivin' okay.

---

7. **accelerates** (uhk-SEL-uh-rayts) *v.* increases speed

Silence. All in the group are looking directly ahead, watching for the point to turn. Other girls adjust their hair, and so forth.

YOUTH

We're coming to that turn-off road. 'Bout 'nother mile.

DRIVER

Tell me before we get there.

(She accelerates again, and the passengers sit up rigidly in response.)

DRIVER

I bet he's got in a big fight.

GIRL

(nervous) Don't go so fast! That turn's right up there. You're gonna' miss it.

DRIVER

No, I won't.

YOUTH

There it is, right up there. Slow down! It's right there.

DRIVER

(shifting down) I see it.

GIRL

Slow down!

There are sounds of grinding gears and squealing tires and all in the car brace for the turn.

DRIVER

(turning steering wheel wildly without direction) . . . I can't see that . . . road!

GIRL

(terror in her voice) Oh, . . . you, stop! We're gonna' wreck!

Others scream as the car goes out of control, sending their bodies flying over the seats. The lights flash in lurches. Crash sounds. Silence. A single shaft of light falls on the Balladeer, who stands atop the embankment, looking first down to the scene, then up and away from it.

BALLADEER
OH, YES, I LOVE YOU HONEY
I DON'T CARE IF YOU'RE MARRIED SIXTEEN TIMES
I STILL LOVE YOU
I'LL GET YOU YET
WHEE YAH HI, WHEE YAH HI UH YO!
OH, YES, I LOVE YOU HONEY
I DON'T CARE IF YOU'RE MARRIED
I WILL DRIVE YOU HOME IN MY ONE-EYED FORD
WHEE YAH HI, WHEE YAH HI UH YO!

Blackout

Scene 10

The girl injured in the car accident lies, apparently dead, on the stage floor. The young tribespeople show no signs of noticing her body. Night Walker is now more intense.

NIGHT WALKER
(to the young people grouped around him) This arbor cannot be killed. It is strong and powerful. It has lived for a very long time. It can be burned and torn apart, but its life cannot be taken from it. It draws its life from the hearts and souls of the tribe, our people.

There was a time in the journey of our people, when the power of the arbor had lost much of its strength.

My grandmother told me the story of this time in our people's journey. An old woman from another place came into the village. She played with the children, who thought she was silly and harmless. She was given a tipi to stay in while she visited.

One night, she invited all of the children of the tribe to her tipi to tell them stories of the land from where she had come.

The children begged her to tell them more; her stories were the kind that young people like to hear.

She told them that if they wanted to go to her country she would take them. They had to promise her that they would do everything that she told them to do. They all agreed.

The smoke from her fire became thick. The old woman told the children to put their hands into the smoke, and the smoke would carry them up through the flap of the tipi and out over the night sky to her land. They agreed to forget all of the ways of our people while they were on the journey.

The children were eager to go to her country. They did as the old lady told them to do, and one by one their figures and voices disappeared from the circle around the fire.

One of the mothers of the tribe went to the tipi to bring her children back to her camp. She cried out when she saw the tipi was empty. The fire was still burning.

The tribespeople became angry. The chiefs had young warriors guard the tipi. A prayer meeting was held. The ceremonial leader sought a vision.

All the tribe crowded around our arbor to hear him tell of what he had seen.

"The children are still in the tipi," the good man told the tribespeople. "The old lady visitor played a trick on them. She promised to take them to her country. But she is the only one who could leave the tipi. The children are safe, they are warm, they are singing and dancing, playing games and telling stories. None of them is quarrelling with the others."

"But the tipi is empty, our children are dead, they have been stolen!" the tribespeople cried out. The mothers began to wail.

"They are in the tipi," the old man repeated.

The people did not believe him. They said his vision was wrong. The chiefs pulled in the horses and formed the braves into groups to search for the lost children. The men rode off, leaving only the old people and the women. The wise man stayed under the arbor, praying.

He prayed for many seasons.

The women would not look at him. They wanted to burn the tipi, but he said they would have to kill him if they did. They were afraid to harm the holy man, and he still prayed.

Then the hunting parties began to return to the camp. The men had ridden far in all directions. Their grief was strong for their lost children. They had changed as men.

None of the tribespeople would come to the arbor.

The wise man saw that the fire, which had not stopped burning, had started to go out.

He carried firewood to the tipi and waited outside until the fire had nearly died out. Some of the tribespeople gathered around to watch. The holy man went into the tipi with the firewood and started the fire again. When the flames began to jump from the burning wood, the wise man started to sing. The smoke began rising up through the flap. Many tribespeople were outside the tipi now, watching and talking among themselves.

Suddenly, many voices could be heard singing, the voices of the children. The singing got louder. From outside the tipi the tribespeople could see in now. They saw the figures of their children take shape through the light. The wise man led the singing children out of the tipi and into the arms of their mothers and fathers. The people cried out in happiness.

The wise man led all the people to the arbor. One of the older boys stood to talk before all of the tribe. "We have been inside the tipi," he said. "We could see all of you, but you could not see us. We could not come out until you believed that we were inside. We sang, danced, used the colors." He showed them a pretty breastplate that he had made. "We have changed," he told the tribe. "We are better men and women now."

Night Walker strikes the drum a single hit, then a second one, and the injured girl rises from the stage floor and joins the group.

The tribespeople painted the tipi with beautiful colors and designs. They placed many gifts under the arbor. The arbor once again was covered with the beautiful light of its love for the people.

Rattles, bells, and drum begin, but lowly.

NIGHT WALKER
  (*directly to the young people*) You will pray at the arbor for

many seasons. Pray for our tribe to gather beneath it.

YOUNG MAN

I will always find the willow branches.

YOUNG WOMAN

And I will place them on the poles.

YOUNG MAN

I will bring the feathers and the ribbons.

YOUNG WOMAN

And I will braid them into the branches.

The arbor comes blazingly alight.

PATROL VOICE 1

Five and 6, you both come through the county road
line, block it off 'bout half a mile down from the
dance grounds. Don't let any of 'em through, not a
car. We'll bottle ever . . . one of 'em up in there.
Seven, 8, and 9, the four of us'll go in from the main
road. All other units in the area'll be in position on 62
and 9. Five and 6, we'll move in when you're sittin'
solid. Over.

Drumbeat rises straight up, then stops.

Scene 11

*T*wo *young men in the 49 group start a violent pushing
and shoving match in the midst of the round dancing. The
drumbeat quickens, and the 49 group forms a semicircle around
the fighters. The Balladeer appears over the scene and sings as the
fight swirls furiously up and down the area.*

BALLADEER
(*as commentary on the fight*)
A HAY HEY A YAH HEY YA HO
A YAH HEY A YAH HEY YA HO
A YAH HEY A HAH HEY YA HO
A YAH HO
A YAH HEY A YAH HEY YO!

A YAH HEY A YAH FIGHT IT OUT!
A YAH HEY A YAH FIGHT IT OUT!
KNOCK HIM OUT! A YAH HEY A YAH HEY YO!

A YAH HEY A YAH CUT HIS HEART!
A YAH HEY A YAH CUT HIS HEART!
A YAH HEY A YAH CUT HIS HEART!
CUT IT OUT! A YAH HEY A YAH HEY YO.

A YAH HEY A YAH TAKE HIS EYE!
A YAH HEY A YAH TAKE HIS EYE!
A YAH HEY A YAH TAKE HIS EYE!
TEAR IT OUT! A YAH HEY A YAH HEY YO.

A YAH HEY A YAH HIT HIM HARD!
A YAH HEY A YAH HIT HIM HARD!
A YAH HEY A YAH KICK HIM HARD!
FIGHT ALL NIGHT! A YAH HEY EY YAH HEY EY HO.

A YAH HEY A YAH HEY YA HO
A YAH HEY A YAH HEY YA HO
A YAH HEY A YAH HEY YA HO
A YA HO
A YAH HEY A YAH HEY YO.

Guys from the crowd separate the two fighters, whose girlfriends push through and take their partners. The crowd breaks up.

VOICE OF 49'ER
(*suddenly, from down the road*) Hi-po's! Cops! Bunch of 'em!

VOICE OF 49'ER
(*from behind*) Hi-po's! On the back road!

ANOTHER VOICE
Hi-po's! Comin' in from both directions!

The 49 stops as response develops. Flashes of patrol car spotlights pierce the dark.

PATROL VOICE 1

(calmly) Unit 4. Unit 4. Units 4 and 6 sittin' solid. We got this back road blocked tight. Looks like they're sittin' solid too.

PATROL VOICE 2

Unit 4 to Units 5 and 6. You read me clear?

PATROL VOICE 1

Five and 6, we read you clear.

PATROL VOICE 2

Don't let a single car, repeat, not a single car, get through. They'll sit solid 'til we show 'em we mean business. Group two and three will move in on call.

PATROL VOICE 1

We read you, Unit 4.

PATROL VOICE 2

I can see a big gang of 'em right down the road where I'm sittin'. Looks like about a hunnerd of 'em, kinda' like they're a-walkin' this way. Keep your toplights on. Over.

The 49 group forms a line of defense across the front of the area, facing the police car lights. One of them emerges as a leader. Their voices deepen, as if they are in a kind of trance, but this is to indicate a sudden new strength.

49'ER

Don't come any further!

ANOTHER 49'ER

You're not taking . . . any . . . of us!

ANOTHER 49'ER

None of us.

Drumbeat paces the action now. Their attitude of resistance becomes firmer.

PATROL VOICE 1

All right, people, let's break it up! Let's go! Let's get these cars outa here. Ever one of you drivin' one of these cars get out your driver's license. Come on! Let's go! Ever'body else get out your I.D. Let's go!

49'ER

You go!

PATROL VOICE 2

We got you from both ends. Ain't a one of you can get out!

49'ER

We don't want out!

PATROL VOICE 1

(*angry*) I said let's go! Let's move it!

(Brief silence. Drumbeat low.)

PATROL VOICE 2

We'll move in on you, people. We'll use gas and bring in the dogs if we have to.

The line is strengthened. The sirens blare. Car lights move up and shine directly in the 49'ers faces. Night Walker, as an apparition,[8] moves close in.

49'ER

You want us. Come and get us!

NIGHT WALKER

(*as a vision*) I see a path not walked on. I hear a song not yet sung. A fire is burning. I smell the cedar. I see the colors strong and shining. There's a circle, round and perfect. A beautiful bird is flying.

---

8. apparition (ap-uh-RIHSH-uhn) *n.* something of someone that appears unexpectedly, a ghost

49'ER

> We'll be here all night!

49'ER

> And all day!

49'ER

> And all night again!

To a powerful drumbeat and in gymnastic movements, they form an elaborate barricade with their bodies, allow the image to strike, then dismantle and form another in the center of the dance circle. Patrol car lights continue to flash.

NIGHT WALKER

> A beautiful bird is flying!

The patrol car lights slowly begin to fade one at a time as the patrols pull back.

49'ER

> We'll leave . . . when we're ready to leave!

BALLADEER

> IT'S GOOD WHERE WE'VE BEEN AND WHERE WE'RE GOING
> HI YI
> HEY YEY HI YI HI YI HI YA-AY HI YI
>
> IF YOU GET LOST JUST KEEP ON MOVING
> HI YI
> HEY YEY HI YI HI YI HI YA-AH HI YI
>
> A BROTHER'S THERE TO WALK BESIDE YOU
> HI YI
> HEY YEY HI YI HI YI HI YA-AY HI YI
>
> YOUR SISTER'S LOVE IS THERE TO GUIDE YOU
> HI YI
> HEY YEY HI YI HI YI HI YA-AY HI YI
>
> IT'S GOOD WHERE WE'VE BEEN AND WHERE WE'RE GOING
> HI YI
> HEY YEY HI YI HI YI HI YA-AY HI YI.

The change from this scene to the next is paced by the rattles.

Scene 12

*F*rom their defensive positions, the 49 group now turns toward the center of the circle, where Night Walker is standing in a shaft of colored light. He is holding a bull-roarer and a rattle.

NIGHT WALKER
I am the oldest man of the tribe!
You have shown me your respect for me.
You will always have mine.

Now, at a carefully measured pace, Night Walker creates the effect of a violent storm as he speaks his final incantation.[9] Each time he spins his bull-roarer, one of the young people is propelled to the center of the circle.

NIGHT WALKER
Go!
Go forward!
The tribe needs you.
I go with you.
I am always with you.
We are a tribe!
Of singers.
Of dancers who move with the grace of the bird.
Of people who know color.
Of weavers.

---

9. incantation (ihn-kan-TAY-shuhn) *n.* the chanting of magic words to cast a spell

Of good hunters.
We pray.
We are a tribe!
Of people with strong hearts.
Who respect fear
As we make our way.
Who will never kill
Another man's way of living.

The sound of his rattle signals the young people to move out to the edges of the circle. The storm is over, and there is a calm.

NIGHT WALKER
I am the oldest man of the tribe!
I heal my sister's child.
I pray for you.
I sing for you.
I smoke for you.
I give to you these things.
You give them life.

A separate drum begins to beat outside the area. The roadway lights up, and the young people sing as they go off in formation.

YOUNG PEOPLE
WALKING DOWN THAT POLLEN ROAD
EVERYTHING IS BEAUTIFUL
WALKING DOWN THAT POLLEN ROAD
EVERYTHING IS BEAUTIFUL

WALKING TO THE EAST
EVERYTHING IS BEAUTIFUL
WALKING TO THE NORTH
EVERYTHING IS BEAUTIFUL
WALKING TO THE WEST
EVERYTHING IS BEAUTIFUL
WALKING TO THE SOUTH
EVERYTHING IS BEAUTIFUL

HEY AH NAH HEY NAY
HEY AH NAH HEY NAY
HEY AH NAH HEY NAY OH

Night Walker is left alone in the dance circle. After a long pause, during which he faces the audience directly, he turns and walks off as he entered. The chant continues as he leaves, and ends as the lights fade slowly. The arbor is left with a special glow. No curtain.

END

AFTER YOU READ

Exchanging Backgrounds and Cultures

1. How do the Weaving Woman and the Singing Man emphasize the importance of the imagination in Native American culture?

2. What does the Night Walker reveal about his people's attitude toward other cultures when he says "We are a tribe!/Of people . . ./Who will never kill/Another man's way of living."? What do the police reveal about their attitude toward other cultures?

3. How do the young people demonstrate their cultural pride and unity in Scene 11 of the play?

What Do You Think?

Which character, scene, or event in the play appealed to you most? Why was it meaningful to you?

Experiencing Drama

In this play, the 49 is a celebration of one's identity and heritage. Think about other types of celebrations, such as weddings, or holidays that you have either participated in or observed. Write a short scene that shows the meaning of the celebration.

Optional Activity Write a short scene about a school event that you and your classmates organized. Like *49*, which describes a situation in which young people come together, your scene should convey how this event united your classmates. Include stage directions that describe how the actors should speak and move and how the stage should look.

UNIT 5: FOCUS ON WRITING

Dramas are meant to be heard and seen. For example, the many Native American chants and dances in Hanay Geiogamah's play, *49,* are intended to be performed on stage in front of an audience.

Writing a Dramatic Sketch

A dramatic sketch has the same form as a full-length drama, but it consists of only one brief scene that makes a single point. Write a dramatic sketch about a historical event, a family gathering, or another topic of your choice.

The Writing Process

Good writing requires both time and effort. An effective writer completes a number of stages that together make up the writing process. The stages of the writing process are given below to help guide you through your assignment.

Prewriting

Once you have chosen your topic, think about the purpose of your sketch. What message or theme would you like to convey? How will the characters, setting, and plot reveal your message?

Decide on a group of characters and make a list of their names. Next to each name, write a brief description of that character. For instance, in Geiogamah's play, the characters are listed in a section called "The People of the Play."

When choosing the setting and events, remember that you must be able to present them on stage. Avoid situations that are difficult to reproduce. Make a list of the movable objects, or props, you will need. Remember that the props and costumes should reflect the time period in which the action occurs. Next, write a brief outline of the plot. How does the play begin? How and when is the central conflict introduced and resolved?

Drafting and Revising

Remember that the first draft of the sketch need not be perfect. You will have an opportunity to revise it later. Your sketch should begin with the list of characters and their descriptions. Following the list of characters, write a set of stage directions that give a detailed description of the setting. The description must be clear and precise enough that the director and actors will know exactly what you intended when you wrote the sketch.

Next, write the dialogue and the stage directions that describe the action of the sketch. You can include some dramatic techniques, such as soliloquies (suh-LIHL-uh-kweez) and asides, to convey information about a character or event. A **soliloquy** is a long speech made by a character who is alone and who reveals his or her private thoughts to the audience. An **aside** is said by an actor to the audience in such a way that the other characters on stage cannot hear.

After you have finished drafting, revise your work. Remember that a dramatic sketch should be brief and make a single point. Therefore, the dialogue and stage directions should directly relate to the purpose of the sketch. Eliminate excessive and unrelated information. Next, read the dialogue aloud with a friend or classmate. Make sure that the dialogue sounds like realistic and natural conversation.

Proofreading and Publishing

Proofread the sketch, correcting any errors in spelling, grammar, punctuation, and capitalization. Then, make a neat final copy.

Now choose actors from among your classmates and perform the play for the teachers and students in your school.

LITERATURE ACKNOWLEDGMENTS

Globe Book Company wishes to thank the following copyright owners for permission to reproduce literature in this book.

ANNETTE ARKEKETA for Annette Arkeketa West, "Calumet Early Evening" from *Prairie* by Annette Arkeketa West, 1978. Reprinted in *That's What She Said: Contemporary Poetry and Fiction by Native American Women,* edited by Rayna Green. Published by Indiana University Press, 1984.

AUNT LUTE BOOKS, (415) 558-8116, for Paula Gunn Allen, "Grandmother" from the chapter, "The Bearer of the Sun Arises" in *The Woman Who Owned the Shadows.* Copyright (c) 1983 by Paula Gunn Allen.

FIREBRAND BOOKS, Ithaca, New York, for Anna Lee Walters, adaptation of "The Warriors" from *The Sun Is Not Merciful.* Copyright (c) 1985 by Anna Lee Walters.

JOY HARJO for Joy Harjo, "Morning Once More" from *What Moon Drove Me To This?* Copyright 1979 Joy Harjo. Reprinted by permission of Joy Harjo.

HARPERCOLLINS PUBLISHERS for N. Scott Momaday, "The Priest of the Sun" from *House Made of Dawn* by N. Scott Momaday. Copyright (c) 1966, 1967, 1968 by N. Scott Momaday. Reprinted by permission of HarperCollins Publishers.

LANCE HENSON for Lance Henson, "Extinction" from *Keeper of Arrows: Poems for the Cheyenne.* Copyright (c) 1970, 1971 Lance Henson.

HENRY HOLT AND COMPANY, INC., for Louise Erdrich, "Indian Boarding School: The Runaways" from *Jacklight.* Copyright (c) 1984 by Louise Erdrich.

DONALD MILLER, agent for John Trudell, for John Trudell, "We've Got to Have Commitment So Strong..." from *Akwesasne Notes,* Early Summer (July issue) 6:3, 1974. Copyright (c) 1974 John Trudell.

PANTHEON BOOKS, a division of Random House, Inc., for Lenard Crow Dog, "Remaking the World" from *American Indian Myths and Legends,* selected and edited by Richard Erdoes and Alfonso Ortiz. Recorded by Richard Erdoes. Copyright (c) 1984 by Richard Erdoes and Alfonso Ortiz.

CARTER REVARD for Carter Revard, "Driving in Oklahoma" from *Nimrod*, 1972-1973. Reprinted in *Ponca War Dancers*, Point Riders Press, 1980; and in *Harper's Anthology of 20th Century Native American Poetry*, edited by Duane Niatum, Harper & Row, Publishers, 1988. Copyright (c) 1972 Carter Revard.

THUNDER'S MOUTH PRESS for Joy Harjo, "Remember" from *She Had Some Horses*. Copyright (c) 1983 by Thunder's Mouth Press.

UNIVERSITY OF NEBRASKA PRESS for Black Elk, excerpt from *Black Elk Speaks: Being the Life Story of a Holy Man of the Ogalala Sioux*, as told to John G. Neihardt. University of Nebraska Press. Copyright 1932, 1959, 1972, by John G. Neihardt. Copyright (c) 1961 by the John G. Neihardt Trust.

UNIVERSITY OF OKLAHOMA PRESS for Hanay Geiogamah, excerpts from "49" from *New Native American Drama: Three Plays* by Hanay Geiogamah. Copyright (c) 1980 by the University of Oklahoma Press. / Madonna Swan, excerpts from *Madonna Swan: A Lakota Woman's Story* by Mark St. Pierre. Copyright (c) 1991 by Mark St. Pierre. Reprinted by permission of the University of Oklahoma Press.

JAMES WELCH for James Welch, "The Man From Washington" from *Riding the Earthboy 40*. Copyright (c) by James Welch.

NOTE: The following story is in the public domain: "The School Days of an Indian Girl," by Zitkala-Ša, from *American Indian Stories*.

ART ACKNOWLEDGMENTS

cover and p. 91: Prairie Fire, Blackbear Bosin, *Philbrook Museum of Art*, Tulsa, Oklahoma

p. 3: Buffalo Hide, *Smithsonian Institute*, Neg # 31155E

p. 39: Shield, State Museum, Oklahoma Historical Society, Oklahoma City, 166

p. 57: Mirror and case, *Philbrook Museum of Art*, Tulsa, Oklahoma, gift of Mrs. Mark Dunlop, 78.8

P. 107: Arapaho Ghost Dance Shirt, National Museum of the American Indian, *Smithsonian Institution 2/1133*